ASIA BOND MONITOR
NOVEMBER 2024

SIAN DEVELOPMENT BANK

Contents

Emerging East Asian Local Currency Bond Markets: A Regional Update

Executive Summary

Recent Developments in Financial Conditions in Emerging East Asia

Financial conditions in emerging East Asia slightly weakened from 2 September to 31 October.[1] While financial conditions improved in September amid monetary easing in advanced and some regional economies, this trend was interrupted in October over uncertainty in the United States (US) Federal Reserve's monetary easing path (following stronger September labor market data) and US elections. Thus, while short-term sovereign bond yields largely declined following policy rate cuts in some regional markets, 10-year sovereign bond yields rose in most regional markets.

Key financial indicators in most regional financial markets slightly weakened during the review period. Regional currencies depreciated by a simple average of 0.7% and a gross-domestic-product-weighted average of 0.3%. Risk premiums, captured by the credit default swap spread, rose by 2.8 basis points (simple average) and 6.1 basis points (gross-domestic-product-weighted average). Excluding the People's Republic of China (PRC), regional equity markets gained 6.2% (market-weighted average) during the review period, with even larger gains recorded in the PRC (16.7%) and Hong Kong, China (14.8%) in response to stimulus measures. During the review period, both regional equity and bond markets recorded net portfolio outflows.

Risks to the regional financial conditions remain balanced. On the upside, moderating inflation and ongoing monetary easing by major advanced economies and many regional central banks are supporting financial conditions. On the downside, there are uncertainties over the Federal Reserve's monetary easing pace, and policy adjustments by the new US administration such as possible larger budget deficits and higher tariffs, which may affect the economic outlook and inflation path. Other downside risks include weaker-than-expected economic growth in the PRC, escalating geopolitical tensions in the Middle East, potential trade tensions between major regional trade partners, and extreme weather that could affect agricultural output and drive up inflation.

Recent Developments in Local Currency Bond Markets in Emerging East Asia

Local currency (LCY) bonds outstanding in emerging East Asia totaled USD26.8 trillion at the end of September, expanding 2.7% quarter-on-quarter (q-o-q) on robust issuance and exceeding the 2.1% q-o-q growth in the previous quarter. Government bonds outstanding rose 3.7% q-o-q to reach USD16.9 trillion at the end of the third quarter (Q3) of 2024, largely buoyed by accelerated growth in the PRC bond market as the government raised funds to finance stimulus measures. The region's outstanding corporate bonds rose 0.8% q-o-q to USD9.2 trillion amid increased corporate financing activities as financial conditions improved. LCY bonds outstanding in Association of Southeast Asian Nations (ASEAN) markets tallied USD2.5 trillion at the end of September, accounting for 9.5% of total emerging East Asian LCY bonds outstanding.

LCY bond issuance in emerging East Asia rose 11.3% q-o-q and 12.8% year-on-year in Q3 2024 to reach USD3.0 trillion, with both the government and corporate segments registering increased issuance amid improved financial conditions. Government bond issuance surged 20.1% q-o-q to reach USD1.3 trillion, largely driven by sovereign debt issuance in the PRC. Corporate bond issuance rose 9.1% q-o-q to USD975.8 billion on lower borrowing costs and improved financial conditions. Aggregate LCY bond issuance among ASEAN markets totaled USD661.8 billion in Q3 2024, comprising 22.2% of the emerging East Asian total.

---

[1] Emerging East Asia is defined to include member states of the Association of Southeast Asian Nations plus the People's Republic of China; Hong Kong, China; and the Republic of Korea.

A majority of outstanding emerging East Asian Treasury bonds have medium- to long-term tenors and are held by long-horizon institutional investors. At the end of September, securities with remaining maturities of longer than 5 years comprised 54.0% of the region's total outstanding Treasury bonds. The size-weighted average tenor of outstanding Treasury bonds was 9.0 years for emerging East Asia, slightly longer than the corresponding averages for the European Union 20 (EU-20) (8.6 years) and the US (8.2 years). Long-horizon institutional investors, such as banks and insurance and pension funds, remained the primary holders of LCY Treasury bonds in emerging East Asia. Banks held around 35.5% of regional outstanding Treasuries, followed by insurance and pension funds with 28.7%.

Recent Developments in ASEAN+3 Sustainable Bond Markets

ASEAN+3's sustainable bond market posted strong growth in Q3 2024 to reach a size of USD893.1 billion at the end of September.[2] ASEAN+3's q-o-q expansion of 4.1% outpaced that of the EU-20 (1.9%) and the US (1.2%). The market's expansion was largely buoyed by robust quarterly issuance on improved financial conditions. Within ASEAN+3, Hong Kong, China (11.6%) and the member markets of ASEAN (9.2%) posted the fastest q-o-q growth rates. At the end of September, ASEAN+3 continued to have the second-largest regional sustainable bond market in the world with an 18.9% global share, trailing only the EU-20's 36.4%. Despite rapid expansion, the sustainable bond market in ASEAN+3 only comprised 2.3% of its general bond market at the end of September, which was lower than the EU-20's corresponding share of 7.9%.

Sustainable bond issuance in ASEAN+3 rose to a record-high level of USD73.7 billion in Q3 2024 on 42.0% q-o-q growth, up from 3.5% q-o-q in the previous quarter. Increased issuance was fueled by improved financial conditions, which in turn were driven by monetary easing. As a result, ASEAN+3's share of global issuance rose to 31.9% in Q3 2024 from 23.2% in the prior quarter. While LCY financing comprised 67.7% of ASEAN+3 sustainable bond issuance in Q3 2024, this was well below the 94.6% share in its general bond market in the same period. In ASEAN economies, however, LCY financing is broadly similar in both the sustainable bond market (68.1%) and the general bond market (70.8%). Sustainable bond issuance with maturities longer than 5 years comprised a share of 28.8% in ASEAN+3 in Q3 2024 compared with 58.9% in ASEAN, partly due to the strong participation of the public sector in the latter market. Public sector participation contributed to a longer size-weighted average maturity of 14.1 years for ASEAN sustainable bond issuance in Q3 2024, compared with 6.7 years for ASEAN+3 and 7.6 years for the EU-20.

---

[2] ASEAN+3 is defined to include member states of ASEAN plus the People's Republic of China; Hong Kong, China; Japan; and the Republic of Korea.

Developments in Regional Financial Conditions

Emerging East Asian financial conditions slightly weakened between 2 September and 31 October as the monetary easing of major central banks was offset by rising uncertainty about the trajectory of the United States (US) monetary policy (**Table A**).[1] Regional financial conditions improved in September with the start of the US Federal Reserve's easing cycle, which was followed by easing of some regional central banks. However, uncertainties around succeeding rate cuts by the Federal Reserve and policy adjustments by the new US administration, as well as rising geopolitical tensions, weighed on regional financial conditions. These risks are clouding the outlook for the region's financial conditions. During the review period, local currency bond yields at the short-end fell in most regional bond markets, tracking rate cuts by regional central banks, while 10-year yields mostly rose following the rise in US bond yields and amid uncertainties related to the Federal Reserve's easing and US elections. Most regional currencies marginally depreciated against the US dollar, and credit default swap (CDS) spreads slightly widened. During the review period, regional equity and bond markets recorded net portfolio outflows due to large net outflows from major regional markets.

Bond yield movements in advanced economies echoed the uncertainty mentioned above. US yields rose despite the September rate cut, while euro area yields fell and Japanese yields ticked up following their respective central bank policy decisions.

In the US, gradual monetary easing is expected. The Federal Reserve cut the policy rate by 50 basis points (bps) during its 17–18 September Federal Open Market Committee (FOMC) meeting, noting that inflation was on track to sustainably reach the 2.0% target and the labor market had slightly weakened. Most Federal Reserve officials have expressed their preference for a gradual pace of monetary policy easing in the coming meetings this year. For example, Minneapolis Federal Reserve Bank President Neel Kashkari said on 23 September that he expects smaller rate cuts in the future. Federal Reserve Bank of

Table A: Changes in Financial Conditions in Major Advanced Economies and Select Emerging East Asian Markets from 2 September to 31 October 2024

	2-Year Government Bond Yield (bps)	10-Year Government Bond Yield (bps)	5-Year Credit Default Swap Spread (bps)	Equity Index (%)	FX Rate (%)
Major Advanced Economies					
Euro Area	(14)	5	–	(2.9)	(1.7)
Japan	7	4	0.6	(0.6)	(3.4)
United States	25	38	–	1.0	–
Select Emerging East Asian Markets					
People's Republic of China	(0.8)	0.2	7	16.7	(0.01)
Hong Kong, China	26	20	–	14.8	0.3
Indonesia	(2)	18	2	(1.6)	(1.1)
Republic of Korea	(12)	(3)	2	(4.7)	(2.8)
Malaysia	15	16	4	(4.5)	(0.5)
Philippines	(37)	(20)	3	3.2	(3.0)
Singapore	12	8	–	2.8	(1.0)
Thailand	(11)	(15)	2	8.3	1.4
Viet Nam	(2)	(2)	0.1	(1.5)	(1.6)

( ) = negative, – = not available, bps = basis points, FX = foreign exchange.

Note: FX rates are presented against the United States dollar. A positive (negative) value for the FX rate indicates the appreciation (depreciation) of the local currency against the United States dollar.

Source: *AsianBondsOnline* calculations based on Bloomberg LP data.

---

[1] Emerging East Asia is defined to include member states of the Association of Southeast Asian Nations plus the People's Republic of China; Hong Kong, China; and the Republic of Korea.

St. Louis President Alberto Musalem and Federal Reserve Bank of Dallas President Lorie Logan also advocated for a slower pace of rate cuts in the future. On 30 September, Federal Reserve Chair Jerome Powell reiterated that it is unlikely that future rate cuts would be as large as the 50 bps cut in September and, if the economy evolves as expected, to expect two smaller rate cuts by year-end.

Meanwhile, there are lingering concerns about inflation among some Federal Reserve officials, heightening uncertainty over the monetary policy path. On 18 October, Federal Reserve Bank of Atlanta President Raphael Bostic indicated that he favors patience to avoid potentially derailing the disinflation process. On 24 October, Federal Reserve Bank of Cleveland President Beth Hammack mentioned that while progress on inflation has been made, inflation remained above the Federal Reserve's 2.0% goal. During the September FOMC meeting, the median federal funds rate forecast was lowered to 4.4% for 2024 and 3.4% for 2025 from 5.1% and 4.1%, respectively, in June. Thus, the Federal Reserve is projecting two more rate cuts of 25 bps each at its November and December monetary policy meetings. Based on the CME FedWatch Tool, the likelihood of a 50 bps rate cut at the November and December FOMC meetings fell from 50.4% and 23.6%, respectively, on 20 September, to 0% and 0%, respectively, on 31 October, while the probability of a 25 bps rate cut at each meeting rose from 49.6% and 26.3%, respectively, to 94.8% and 75.1% (**Figure A**). Policy adjustments by the new US administration may lead to higher budget deficits and increased inflationary pressure, affecting the pace of monetary easing. As widely expected, the Federal Reserve reduced the federal funds rate by 25 bps at its November meeting. In its decision, the Federal Reserve noted some weakening in the labor market and, while moderating, somewhat still elevated inflation. In addition, uncertainty over a December rate cut increased. As projected by the CME FedWatch Tool on 7 November, the likelihood of a 25 bps rate cut in the December meeting fell to 66.6%, while the likelihood of there being no change rose to 31.0%.

While the US economy remains sound, inflation and the labor market's performance will shape the future path of monetary policy. Annualized gross domestic product (GDP) growth for the third quarter (Q3) of 2024 rose to 2.8% due to strong consumer spending, slightly lower compared with the 3.0% expansion in the previous quarter. The composite Purchasing Managers

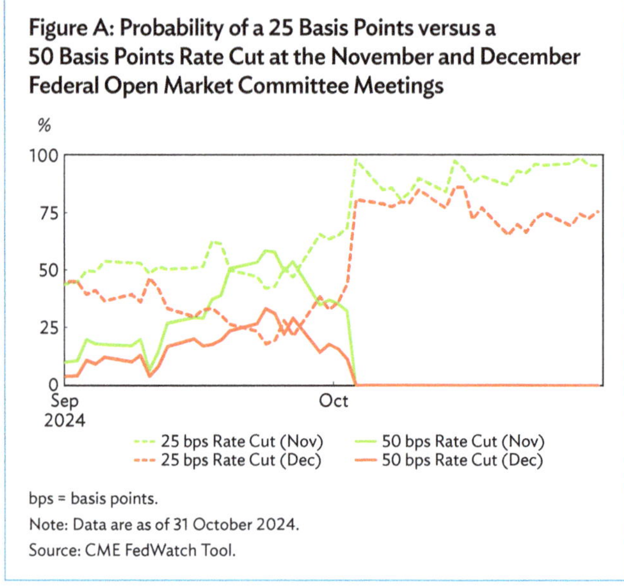

bps = basis points.
Note: Data are as of 31 October 2024.
Source: CME FedWatch Tool.

Index (PMI) remained in expansionary territory at 54.1 and 54.0 in October and September, respectively, albeit slightly lower than 54.6 in August. Consumer price inflation was higher in October at 2.6% year-on-year (y-o-y) versus 2.4% y-o-y in September and 2.5% y-o-y in August, raising further uncertainty over the path of monetary policy. Core consumer price inflation remained unchanged at 3.3% y-o-y in October from September, but was higher than August's 3.2% y-o-y. Nonfarm payroll additions significantly fell in October to 12,000 from 223,000 in September and 78,000 in August, partly driven by recent weather disturbances and labor strikes. The unemployment rate remained at 4.1% in September and October, which was slightly lower than August's reading of 4.2%. The Federal Reserve updated its macroeconomic projections in September, revising GDP growth for 2024 slightly down to an annualized 2.0% from a 2.1% estimate in June, while keeping the 2025 growth forecast unchanged at 2.0%. The 2024 and 2025 Personal Consumption Expenditure inflation forecasts were revised downward to 2.3% and 2.1%, respectively, from June estimates of 2.6% and 2.3%. Unemployment rate forecasts, however, were revised upward to 4.4% for both 2024 and 2025 from 4.0% and 4.2%, respectively, in the June forecasts.

Bond yields in the euro area declined during the review period following two consecutive rate cuts by the European Central Bank (ECB) over subdued economic performance and moderating inflation. On 12 September, the ECB reduced its deposit facility rate by 25 bps for the second time this year, citing that inflation continued to moderate as expected. On 30 September, ECB President Christine Lagarde hinted of another cut at the ECB's October meeting on growing confidence that inflation would fall toward its target path. Many ECB officials noted this too.[2] Some ECB officials supported additional rate cuts over concerns of weakening economic performance in the euro area. On 2 October, ECB Executive Board Member Isabel Schnabel highlighted that headwinds to economic growth could not be ignored, and ECB Vice President Luis de Guindos mentioned that they were in a low-growth environment and that downside risks were high. As widely expected, the ECB reduced key rates by 25 bps at its 17 October monetary policy meeting, noting that economic activity had been weaker than expected.

The ECB's monetary easing path also faces uncertainty. On 22 October, ECB President Christine Lagarde noted that the monetary policy direction of the ECB was clear but that the pace had yet to be determined, with some arguing for a 50 bps rate cut and others calling for a 25 bps rate cut or an even slower pace of easing. For example, Bank of Portugal Governor Mario Centeno and Bank of Latvia Governor Martins Kazaks both indicated on 23 and 24 October, respectively, that a 50 bps rate cut could be considered at the December ECB meeting. Meanwhile, ECB Chief Economist Philip Lane said on 23 October that while the disinflation process was on track, they had not noted any signs of dramatic weakening in the economy. Bank of Estonia Chairman Madis Muller also indicated on 24 October that he was not worried about falling behind the curve.

Economic performance in the euro area remained subdued during the review period. GDP growth ticked slightly higher to 0.9% y-o-y in Q3 2024 from 0.6% y-o-y in the previous quarter. The composite PMI inched up to 50.0 in October from 49.6 in September, but was down from 51.0 in August. The manufacturing PMI in the euro area remained below the 50-point threshold in August, September, and October with readings of 45.8, 45.0, and 46.0, respectively. Inflation in the euro area inched up to 2.0% y-o-y in October from 1.7% y-o-y in September, but was down from 2.6% y-o-y in July and 2.2% y-o-y in August. October's reading fell within the ECB's annual 2.0% target for only the second time during the past 3 years. In September, the ECB slightly revised downward its annual GDP growth forecasts for 2024

and 2025 to 0.8% and 1.3%, respectively, from forecasts of 0.9% and 1.4% in June. However, the ECB expects inflation to rise again by the latter part of this year before it trends downward in the second half of 2025. The ECB's annual inflation forecasts were unchanged for 2024 and 2025 at 2.5% and 2.2%, respectively.

In Japan, bond yields rose during the review period over expectations that the Bank of Japan (BOJ) would continue with monetary tightening, despite uncertainties over the timing. The BOJ left policy rates unchanged at its meeting on 20 September but noted that economic growth remained above potential and inflation is expected to rise in 2025. During the press conference for the 20 September BOJ meeting, Governor Kazuo Ueda mentioned that the BOJ would assess if conditions for further tightening were warranted. On 23 October, BOJ Governor Kazuo Ueda indicated that the appropriate pace and timing of the rate hikes was still being considered, but emphasized it was important not to wait too long. As expected, the BOJ left its policy rate unchanged on 31 October.

Japan's economy remained sound, with some weakening signs in recent economic indicators supporting a possible delay in the expected rate hike. The seasonally adjusted annualized GDP growth rate moderated to 0.9% in Q3 2024 from 2.2% in the second quarter (Q2) of 2024, amid a decline in investments. The labor market however showed improvement, posting an unemployment rate of 2.4% in September from 2.5% in August and 2.7% in July. Meanwhile, Japan's y-o-y inflation eased in September to 2.5% from 3.0% in August, the lowest level since April. However, the manufacturing PMI remained in contractionary territory, reading 49.2 and 49.7 in October and September, respectively, slightly down from 49.8 in August. Industrial production contracted 2.6% y-o-y and 4.9% y-o-y in September and August, respectively, following 2.9% y-o-y growth in July. The BOJ updated its economic forecasts in October, with the annualized GDP growth forecast for 2024 left unchanged at 0.6% but revised slightly up to 1.1% for 2025 from a July estimate of 1.0%. Similarly, the annual consumer price inflation forecast for 2024 was left unchanged at 2.5% but revised down to 1.9% for 2025 from a July estimate of 2.1%.

Local currency bond yields in emerging East Asia largely declined for 2-year tenors during the review period as inflation remained benign and some regional central

---

[2] Several ECB officials noted that a rate cut was forthcoming at the October ECB meeting, including Banque de France Governor Francois Villeroy de Galhau, Bank of Latvia Governor Martins Kazaks, Deutsche Bundesbank President Joachim Nagel, Central Bank of Cyprus Governor Christodoulos Patsalides, and Bank of Greece Governor Yannis Stournaras.

banks began easing monetary policy. In contrast, 10-year yields largely rose, tracking US bond yields, on uncertainties regarding the Federal Reserve's monetary path and US elections. Inflation largely either declined or remained stable across the region. The exception to this trend was the Philippines, where inflation rose to 2.3% y-o-y in October (within the central bank's forecast range of 2.0% to 2.8%) from 1.9% y-o-y in September. Marginal increases were seen in Viet Nam, where inflation rose to 2.9% y-o-y in October from 2.6% y-o-y in September; and in Thailand, where the inflation rate slightly rose to 0.8% y-o-y in October from 0.6% y-o-y in September. The upticks were largely driven by faster increases in food prices in all three markets (**Figure B**).

Among regional central banks, the People's Bank of China (PBOC) and the Bangko Sentral ng Pilipinas (BSP) conducted the most aggressive monetary easing during the review period (**Table B**). On 23 September, the PBOC announced a slew of monetary easing measures,

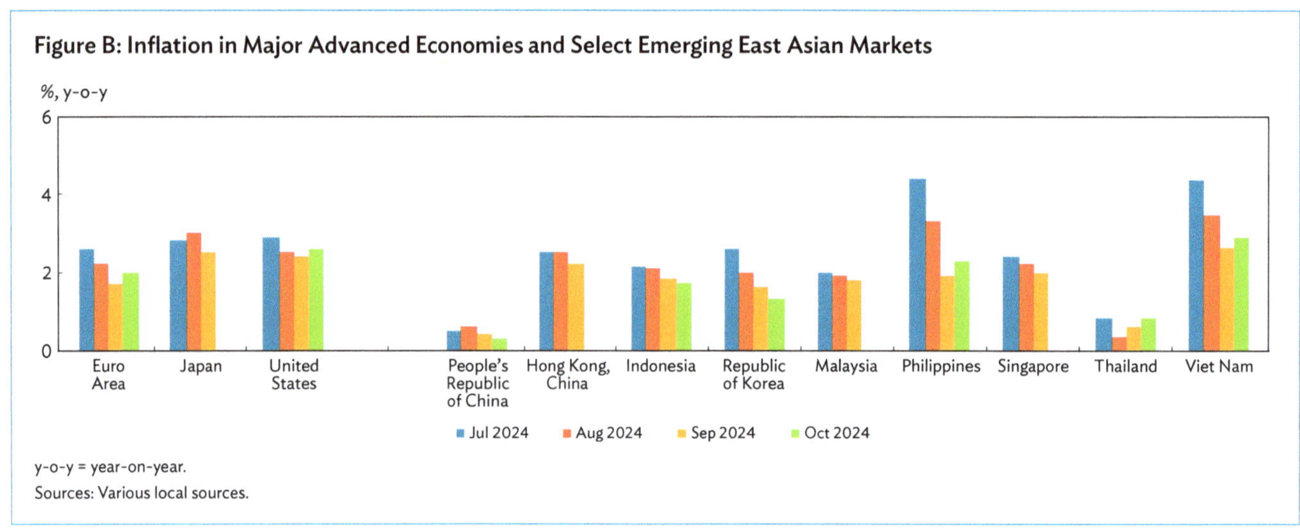

Figure B: Inflation in Major Advanced Economies and Select Emerging East Asian Markets

y-o-y = year-on-year.
Sources: Various local sources.

Table B: Changes in Monetary Stances in Major Advanced Economies and Select Emerging East Asian Markets

Economy	Policy Rate 1-Oct-2023 (%)	Oct-2023	Nov-2023	Dec-2023	Jan-2024	Feb-2024	Mar-2024	Apr-2024	May-2024	Jun-2024	Jul-2024	Aug-2024	Sep-2024	Oct-2024	Policy Rate 31-Oct-2024 (%)	Change in Policy Rates (basis points)
Euro Area	4.00									↓0.25			↓0.25	↓0.25	3.25	↓ 75
Japan	(0.10)						↑0.20				↑0.15				0.25	↑ 35
United Kingdom	5.25											↓0.25			5.00	↓ 25
United States	5.50												↓0.50		5.00	↓ 50
People's Republic of China	2.50									↓0.20			↓0.30		2.00	↓ 50
Indonesia	5.75	↑0.25						↑0.25					↓0.25		6.00	↑ 25
Republic of Korea	3.50													↓0.25	3.25	↓ 25
Malaysia	3.00														3.00	◆ 0
Philippines	6.25	↑0.25										↓0.25		↓0.25	6.00	↓ 25
Singapore	–														–	◆ –
Thailand	2.50													↓0.25	2.25	↓ 25
Viet Nam	4.50														4.50	◆ 0

( ) = negative, ◆ = no change, – = no data.
Notes:
1. Data coverage is from 1 October 2023 to 31 October 2024.
2. For the People's Republic of China, the data used in the chart are for the 1-year medium-term lending facility rate.
3. For the United States, the upper bound of the policy rate target range is reported on the table.
4. The up (down) arrow for Singapore signifies monetary policy tightening (loosening) by its central bank. The Monetary Authority of Singapore utilizes the Singapore dollar nominal effective exchange rate to guide its monetary policy.

Sources: Various central bank websites.

including a 50 bps cut in the reserve requirement ratio and a 20 bps cut in the 7-day reverse repo rate, both of which took effect on 27 September, as well as a 30 bps rate cut in the 1-year medium-term lending facility rate, which took effect on 25 September.[3] Easing price pressures led the BSP to reduce rates by 25 bps each at its August and October meetings. The BSP also announced in September a 250 bps cut in the reserve requirement ratio of universal and commercial banks that took effect on 25 October. Other regional central banks also eased their monetary stances during the review period. Bank Indonesia cut the policy rate by 25 bps on 18 September over moderating inflation. The Bank of Korea cut the policy rate by 25 bps on 11 October amid stable inflation, a weak recovery in domestic demand, and slower GDP growth of 1.5% y-o-y in Q3 2024 versus 2.3% y-o-y in Q2 2024. The Bank of Thailand also reduced the policy rate by 25 bps on 16 October to alleviate the debt servicing burden for borrowers. The State Bank of Vietnam reduced its open market operations interest rate by 25 bps each in August and September to encourage economic activities.

Economic performance in the region slightly weakened, with GDP growth in Q3 2024 moderating in many regional economies. According to the September edition of the *Asian Development Outlook*, the 2024 GDP growth forecast for Southeast Asia was slightly lowered to 4.5% in September from 4.6% in July. This is also in line with the monetary easing stances by many regional central banks. Stronger GDP growth was recorded in Q3 2024 in Singapore due to robust growth in manufacturing and in Viet Nam due to strong consumption (**Table C**). GDP growth in the PRC slightly fell to 4.6% y-o-y in Q3 2024 from 4.7% y-o-y in Q2 2024 over weak domestic demand and slower export growth. GDP growth in both Hong Kong, China and the Republic of Korea declined in Q3 2024 from Q2 2024 due to a weak export performance.

Emerging East Asian currencies were mostly stable, posting a marginal depreciation of 0.3% (GDP-weighted average) and 0.7% (simple average) against the US dollar during the review period. In September, the rate cut by the Federal Reserve led to the collective strengthening of regional currencies by a simple average of 2.0% and

Table C: Gross Domestic Product Growth in Select Emerging East Asian Economies (y-o-y, %)

Economy	2024			Forecast for 2024
	Q1	Q2	Q3	
People's Republic of China	5.30	4.70	4.60	4.80
Hong Kong, China	2.80	3.20	1.80	2.80
Indonesia	5.11	5.05	4.95	5.00
Republic of Korea	3.30	2.30	1.50	2.50
Malaysia	4.20	5.90	5.30	4.50
Philippines	5.80	6.40	5.20	6.00
Singapore	3.00	2.90	4.10	2.60
Thailand	1.60	2.20	3.00	2.30
Viet Nam	5.66	6.93	7.40	6.00

Q1 = first quarter, Q2 = second quarter, Q3 = third quarter, y-o-y = year-on-year.
Notes:
1. Forecasts for 2024 are based on the September 2024 edition of the *Asian Development Outlook*.
2. Q3 2024 data for the Republic of Korea and Singapore are advanced estimates.
Sources: Various local sources.

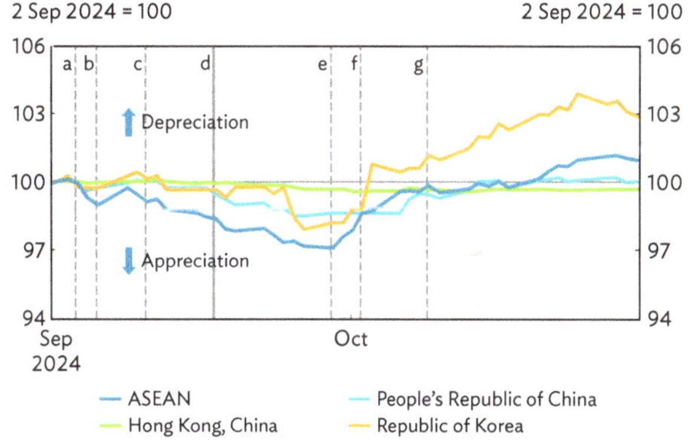

Figure C: Currency Exchange Rate Against the United States Dollar in Select Emerging East Asian Markets

ASEAN = Association of Southeast Asian Nations, US = United States.
a Federal Reserve's beige book shows sluggish and declining economic activity and an uncertain economic outlook.
b Federal Reserve officials Susan Collins and Christopher Waller advocate for more caution in Federal Reserve easing.
c US August inflation falls to 2.5% year on year (y-o-y) from 3.0% y-o-y in July.
d The Federal Reserve reduces its interest rates by 50 basis points to a range of 4.75%–5.00%.
e Federal Reserve Chair Jerome Powell hints at a slower pace of rate cuts in the future.
f Stronger-than-expected US labor market data casts uncertainty on the pace of future rate cuts.
g US September inflation exceeds the forecast of 2.3% y-o-y, stalling disinflation progress.
Notes:
1. ASEAN comprises the markets of Indonesia, Malaysia, the Philippines, Singapore, Thailand, and Viet Nam.
2. Data are as of 31 October 2024.
3. A value higher (lower) than 100 indicates currency depreciation (appreciation) against the US dollar.
Source: *AsianBondsOnline* calculations based on Bloomberg LP data.

---

[3] In the PRC, the PBOC also said that it would guide loan prime rates and deposit rates lower but has yet to set a date. The PBOC also announced that it will reduce rates on existing home loans and standardize the minimum down payment ratio for home loans. Further measures were announced on 12 October and 18 October, including an additional CNY2.3 trillion special bond quota for local governments, a one-time raise in local governments' debt ceiling, issuance of special sovereign bonds to strengthen the regulatory capital of state-owned banks, a share buy-back facility, and an equity swap facility, among others.

a GDP-weighted average of 1.6%. However, regional currencies weakened following the release of strong US labor market data for September on 3 October (**Figure C**). Heightened uncertainties over the future monetary easing path of the Federal Reserve and US elections led to the depreciation of regional currencies versus the US dollar in October by 2.3% (simple average) and 1.9% (GDP-weighted average). During the review period, the Thai baht posted the largest appreciation, gaining 1.4% over improving investor sentiment following the establishment of the new Thai government. In contrast, the Philippine peso weakened by 3.0% as the BSP was among the most aggressive in monetary easing in the region. Following its second rate cut of the year on 16 October, BSP Governor Eli Remolona said there was still room for a third 25 bps rate cut at the central bank's Monetary Board meeting in December. The Korean won weakened by 2.8% partly due to capital outflows from the Republic of Korea's equity market.

Uncertainty in the US monetary easing path marginally pushed up risk premiums in emerging East Asian markets from 2 September to 31 October (**Figure D**). Excluding the PRC, the region's CDS spreads—both the simple average and GDP-weighted average—marginally widened by 2.1 bps during the review period. Meanwhile, the CDS spread in the PRC rose by 7.0 bps on a weak economic performance, widening the regional CDS spread by 2.8 bps (simple average) and 6.1 bps (GDP-weighted average).

CDS spreads rose in all regional economies in October, with the exception of Indonesia, due to heightened uncertainty over the Federal Reserve's monetary policy path and US elections. Indonesia's CDS spread narrowed by 0.3 bps in October as investor concerns about the fiscal policy of the new administration abated. This partly reversed a widening of the risk premium in Indonesia in September over concerns that the new administration would increase borrowing to support fiscal spending. In the PRC, risk premiums rose in both September and October on a weak economic outlook.

Regional equity markets posted gains during the review period. Gains were seen mostly in September while markets posted losses in October following the release of stronger-than-expected labor market data in the US in October as well as regional net portfolio outflows in October. Excluding the PRC, regional equity markets gained 2.1% (simple average) and 6.2% (market-weighted average), supported by monetary easing in both advanced economies and domestic markets. The largest gains were seen in the PRC (16.7%) and Hong Kong, China (14.8%) following easing measures enacted by the PBOC and announcements of stimulus measures in the PRC in September and October (**Figure E**). Thailand saw the region's next largest equity market gains during the review period at 8.3% as investor sentiment improved with the establishment of a new government, release of cash handouts, and launch of a state investment fund.

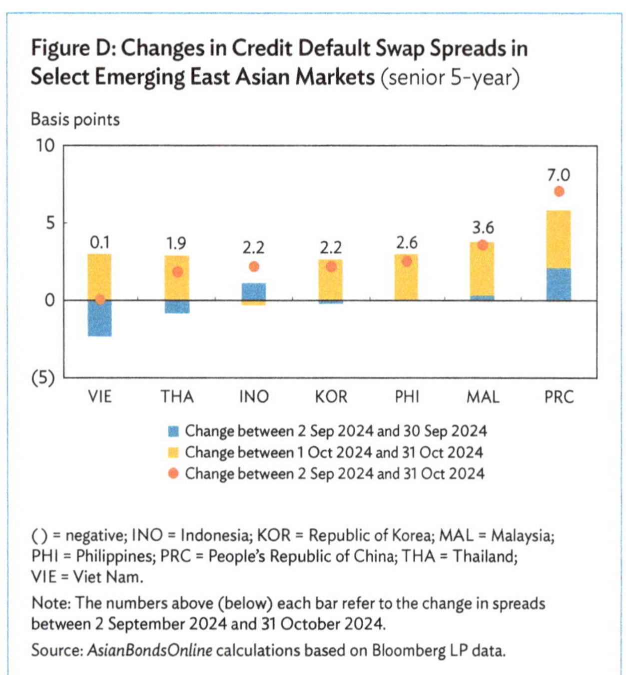

Figure D: Changes in Credit Default Swap Spreads in Select Emerging East Asian Markets (senior 5-year)

( ) = negative; INO = Indonesia; KOR = Republic of Korea; MAL = Malaysia; PHI = Philippines; PRC = People's Republic of China; THA = Thailand; VIE = Viet Nam.
Note: The numbers above (below) each bar refer to the change in spreads between 2 September 2024 and 31 October 2024.
Source: *AsianBondsOnline* calculations based on Bloomberg LP data.

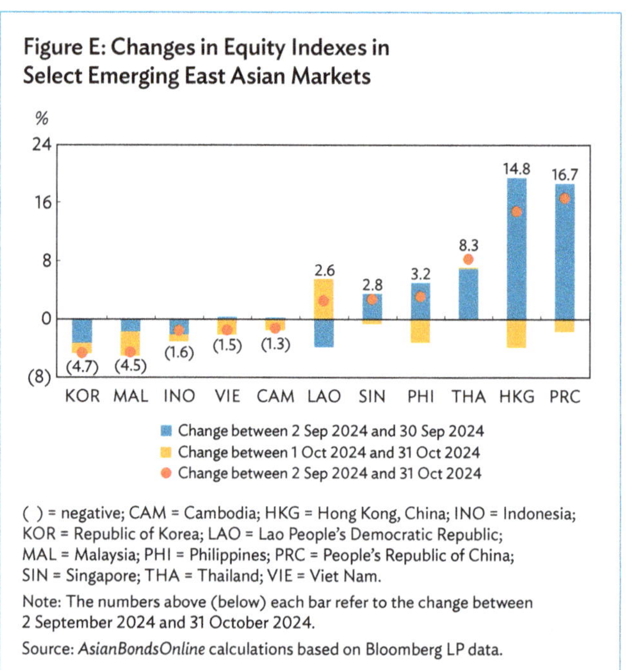

Figure E: Changes in Equity Indexes in Select Emerging East Asian Markets

( ) = negative; CAM = Cambodia; HKG = Hong Kong, China; INO = Indonesia; KOR = Republic of Korea; LAO = Lao People's Democratic Republic; MAL = Malaysia; PHI = Philippines; PRC = People's Republic of China; SIN = Singapore; THA = Thailand; VIE = Viet Nam.
Note: The numbers above (below) each bar refer to the change between 2 September 2024 and 31 October 2024.
Source: *AsianBondsOnline* calculations based on Bloomberg LP data.

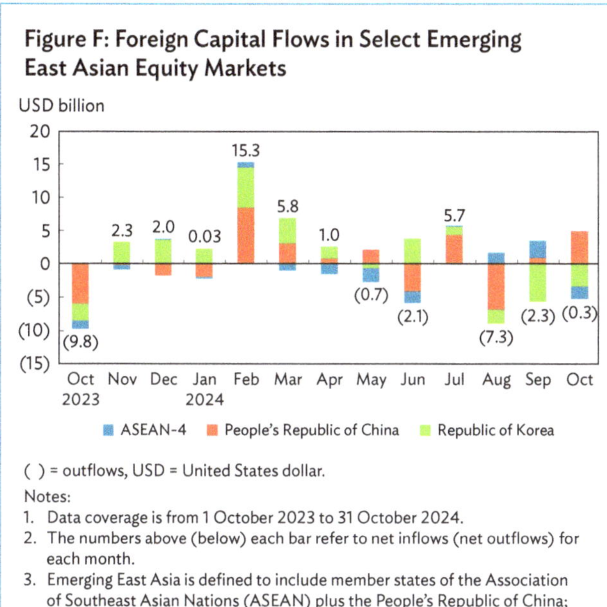

Figure F: Foreign Capital Flows in Select Emerging East Asian Equity Markets

( ) = outflows, USD = United States dollar.
Notes:
1. Data coverage is from 1 October 2023 to 31 October 2024.
2. The numbers above (below) each bar refer to net inflows (net outflows) for each month.
3. Emerging East Asia is defined to include member states of the Association of Southeast Asian Nations (ASEAN) plus the People's Republic of China; Hong Kong, China; and the Republic of Korea.
4. ASEAN-4 includes Indonesia, the Philippines, Thailand, and Viet Nam.
Source: Institute of International Finance.

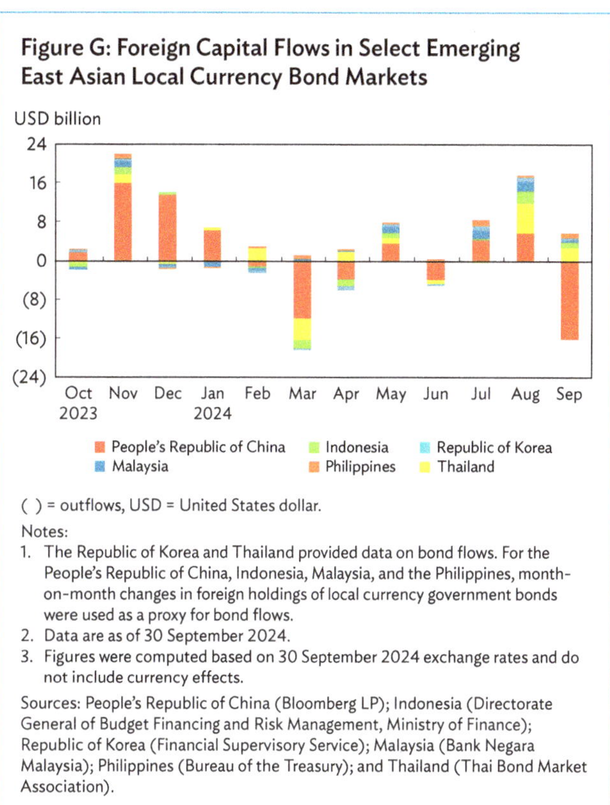

Figure G: Foreign Capital Flows in Select Emerging East Asian Local Currency Bond Markets

( ) = outflows, USD = United States dollar.
Notes:
1. The Republic of Korea and Thailand provided data on bond flows. For the People's Republic of China, Indonesia, Malaysia, and the Philippines, month-on-month changes in foreign holdings of local currency government bonds were used as a proxy for bond flows.
2. Data are as of 30 September 2024.
3. Figures were computed based on 30 September 2024 exchange rates and do not include currency effects.

Sources: People's Republic of China (Bloomberg LP); Indonesia (Directorate General of Budget Financing and Risk Management, Ministry of Finance); Republic of Korea (Financial Supervisory Service); Malaysia (Bank Negara Malaysia); Philippines (Bureau of the Treasury); and Thailand (Thai Bond Market Association).

Regional equity markets recorded net outflows during the review period, driven largely by outflows from the Republic of Korea. In September, net inflows were recorded in the equity markets of ASEAN (USD2.5 billion) and the PRC (USD0.9 billion) amid monetary easing in advanced economies and some regional markets. In October, ASEAN markets posted net portfolio outflows (USD1.9 billion) due to heightened uncertainties over the Federal Reserve's monetary policy path and US elections while the PRC recorded net portfolio inflows (USD5.0 billion) on investor optimism over its stimulus measures. Meanwhile, the Republic of Korea was adversely affected by negative sentiments surrounding the AI industry and lower-than-expected GDP growth, leading to net outflows in both September (USD5.7 billion) and October (USD3.4 billion) (**Figure F**).

In September, regional bond markets recorded net outflows, largely due to outflows from the PRC. Easing monetary policies and moderating inflation generated capital inflows in the rest of the region's bond markets in September (**Figure G**). All regional bond markets, excluding the PRC, posted net portfolio inflows in September amounting to USD5.8 billion on improved investor sentiment over declining inflation across the region and monetary easing in advanced economies. In contrast, the PRC reported net outflows of USD16.1 billion as low yields and economic stimulus prompted investors to shift to equity markets.

Risks to the region's financial conditions outlook remain balanced. On the upside, anticipated easing by central banks throughout the region and in advanced economies is expected to lower borrowing costs and improve financial conditions. This, in turn, will help boost investor confidence and promote economic activities. The regional economy remains robust, and inflation is continuing to moderate. Additionally, a La Niña climate event beginning later this year could create favorable growing conditions for crops, potentially lowering global food prices. These factors are contributing to expectations of continued monetary easing in the region.

There are also several downside risks to the region's financial conditions. In the US, there is uncertainty regarding the pace of the Federal Reserve's monetary easing. The recent strong US labor market data contributed to a less dovish view of future Federal Reserve decisions. A more gradual easing cycle in the US could contribute to monetary policy divergence between the Federal Reserve and regional central banks, heightening uncertainty over exchange rates, capital flows, and asset prices. There is also uncertainty surrounding the policies of the new US administration. The new administration may run higher budget deficits and escalate trade tensions with major regional economies, which may affect the economic outlook and the future inflation path.

Within the region, uncertainty centers around a possible weaker-than-expected economic performance in the PRC. Given close trade ties, this might deter foreign investment and weaken trade performance in other regional markets, possibly dampening consumer and investor sentiment.

Geopolitical tensions in the Middle East are also casting uncertainty on global financial conditions. Inflationary pressures could rise with the possible further disruption to shipping routes and subsequent rise in oil and commodity prices. Moreover, extreme weather from a La Niña event would increase the risk of flooding and landslides, threatening agriculture and livelihoods, which could potentially push up food prices and slow monetary easing in the region. Climate risks also threaten the fiscal space of the economy, as discussed in the **Box**.

Box: Mitigating the Sovereign Credit Risk Impact of Climate Vulnerability

Climate risks, which refer to the potential adverse socioeconomic impacts of climate change, entail substantial fiscal risks, especially through their adverse effects on fiscal space. For instance, a major disaster due to climate change is likely to necessitate large fiscal outlays for relief and recovery efforts; or, extreme heat resulting from global warming may cause extensive agricultural damage, forcing governments to provide subsidies to hard-hit farmers. At a broader level, public spending on climate change adaptation and mitigation looms as one of the biggest sources of fiscal demands around the world. In combination with other large looming fiscal demands, such as those related to population aging, climate-change-related fiscal expenditures pose a major threat to fiscal space and fiscal sustainability in the future.

Beirne, Park, Saadaoui, and Uddin (2024) examine the impact of climate risks on fiscal space across a sample of 199 economies over the period 1990 to 2022. To measure fiscal space, the paper uses both sovereign bond yields and ratings on foreign-currency, long-term sovereign debt. Higher sovereign bond yields and lower sovereign debt ratings imply higher borrowing costs and default risks, and shrinking fiscal space.

The paper also examines the role of political stability and financial development in mitigating such climate-related fiscal risks. That is, it investigates whether politically more stable and financially more developed economies are less vulnerable to climate-related fiscal risks. Political stability is likely to mitigate these risks since it increases the likelihood of more sustainable fiscal policy—for example, in the form of a more

robust medium-term fiscal framework. As a result, a more stable political environment is likely to reduce the impact of climate shocks and other shocks on fiscal sustainability.

In addition, political stability is conducive to more careful, rational, and cost-effective government planning in response to potential climate shocks, which will help to preserve fiscal space. Financial development is also expected to mitigate climate-related fiscal risks. In particular, in a financially well-developed economy, firms and households will have access to insurance and other financial instruments that protect them from the negative effects of climate shocks. This, in turn, reduces the need for large fiscal outlays and thus mitigates the negative effect on fiscal space. Furthermore, financial development increases the amount of credit available to firms and households to help them cushion the impact of potential climate shocks.

Using panel local projections to estimate the response of sovereign bond yields to climate vulnerability, conditioning on political stability and financial development, the paper finds a significant mitigating role for economies that are more politically stable and have higher levels of financial development. As shown in **Figure B.1**, a one-unit rise in climate vulnerability leads to a statistically significant 1 percentage point rise in bond yields where political stability risks are elevated, with the peak effect at 2 years after the shock. On the other hand, the response of bond yields has no statistically significant impact where political stability risks are more muted. In the case of financial development, as shown in **Figure B.2**, economies with low levels of financial

This box was written by John Beirne (principal economist) and Donghyun Park (economic advisor) of the Asian Development Bank, Jamel Saadaoui (full professor) at the University of Paris 8, and Gazi Salah Uddin (associate professor) at Linkoping University.

continued on next page

Box *continued*

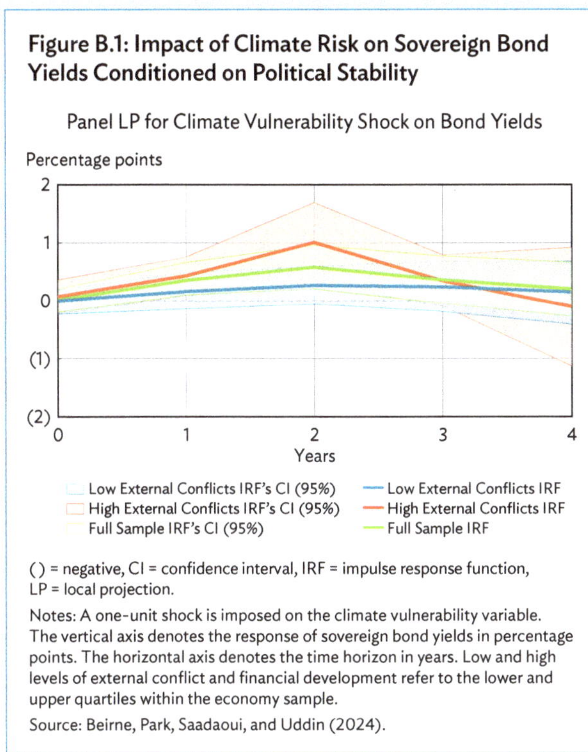

Figure B.1: Impact of Climate Risk on Sovereign Bond Yields Conditioned on Political Stability

Panel LP for Climate Vulnerability Shock on Bond Yields

Percentage points

( ) = negative, CI = confidence interval, IRF = impulse response function, LP = local projection.

Notes: A one-unit shock is imposed on the climate vulnerability variable. The vertical axis denotes the response of sovereign bond yields in percentage points. The horizontal axis denotes the time horizon in years. Low and high levels of external conflict and financial development refer to the lower and upper quartiles within the economy sample.

Source: Beirne, Park, Saadaoui, and Uddin (2024).

Figure B.2: Impact of Climate Risk on Sovereign Bond Yields Conditioned on Financial Development

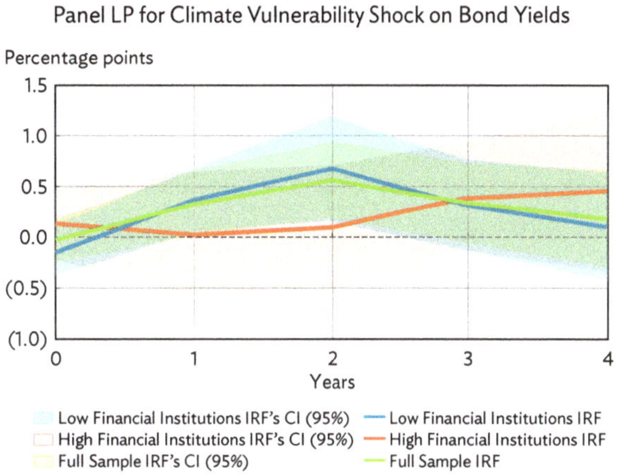

Panel LP for Climate Vulnerability Shock on Bond Yields

Percentage points

( ) = negative, CI = confidence interval, IRF = impulse response function, LP = local projection.

Notes: A one-unit shock is imposed on the climate vulnerability variable. The vertical axis denotes the response of sovereign bond yields in percentage points. The horizontal axis denotes the time horizon in years. Low and high levels of external conflict and financial development refer to the lower and upper quartiles within the economy sample.

Source: Beirne, Park, Saadaoui, and Uddin (2024).

development have greater susceptibility to climate-related sovereign risks. Bond yields rise by around 0.6 percentage points for these economies, with a peak effect at 2 years after the shock. Meanwhile, where financial development is high, no significant effect is found.

Overall, the empirical analysis indicates that climate vulnerability adversely affects fiscal space and that the effects are most pronounced in economies that are most vulnerable to climate change, as well as where fiscal space is most constrained. Moreover, it is found that these effects are alleviated in economies with more stable political environments and better developed financial markets.

More precisely, the evidence indicates that climate risks are associated with lower bond risk premiums, as well as higher sovereign ratings, in economies that suffer less from both external and internal conflict. In addition, better financial development weakens the link between climate risks and fiscal space. Financially more developed economies do

not experience a climate-related bond risk premium or a persistent deterioration of sovereign ratings due to climate vulnerability.

While fiscal consolidation is the key to mitigate the adverse effect of climate risks on fiscal space, both political stability and financial development can contribute as well. Political stability is desirable in and of itself, but it can also yield a significant additional benefit in the form of shielding fiscal space from climate risk. Similarly, the results strengthen the case for governments to further promote financial development.

Reference

J. Beirne, D. Park, J. Saadaoui, and G. Salah Uddin. 2024. Impact of Climate Risk on Fiscal Space: Do Political Stability and Financial Development Matter? *ADB Economics Working Paper*. No. 748. Asian Development Bank.

Bond Market Developments in the Third Quarter of 2024

Section 1. Local Currency Bonds Outstanding

The emerging East Asian local currency (LCY) bond market continued to expand in the third quarter (Q3) of 2024, reaching a size of USD26.8 trillion at the end of September.[4] The region's LCY bond market saw a year-on-year (y-o-y) expansion of 8.2% in Q3 2024, which exceeded the corresponding y-o-y growth rates in the United States (US) market (6.8%) and the European Union 20 (EU-20) (4.8%). At the end of September, the size of the emerging East Asian LCY bond market was equivalent to 67.5% of the US market (USD39.6 trillion) and 118.3% of the EU-20 market (USD22.6 trillion) (**Figure 1**).

Robust issuance of government and corporate bonds in the People's Republic of China (PRC), due in part to monetary policy easing by the central bank, helped prop up emerging East Asian LCY bond market growth in Q3 2024. Quarterly growth in LCY bonds outstanding picked up in Q3 2024, rising to 2.7% quarter-on-quarter (q-o-q) from 2.1% q-o-q in the second quarter (Q2) (**Table 1**). The growth in LCY Treasury bonds climbed to 3.7% q-o-q in Q3 2024 from 2.8% in Q2 2024, largely buoyed by the PRC, while several of the region's governments eased debt issuance during the quarter as they had already raised funds during the first half of the year. The stock of LCY corporate bonds rose 0.8% q-o-q in Q3 2024, up from 0.6% q-o-q in the previous quarter, supported by increased issuance in the PRC. Financial corporations in the PRC continued to raise funds to comply with regulatory capital requirements, while monetary policy easing by the People's Bank of China (PBOC) helped facilitate increased issuance of nonfinancial corporate bonds. Overall, most of the region's markets saw positive q-o-q growth in Q3 2024, with only Hong Kong, China posting a contraction as a relatively large volume of its government bonds matured during the quarter (**Figure 2**). LCY bonds outstanding in Association of Southeast Asian Nations (ASEAN) markets rose 2.3% q-o-q during the quarter, with Indonesia and the Philippines recording the fastest growth among emerging East Asian markets in Q3 2024.

The ASEAN LCY bond market rose to a size of USD2.5 trillion at the end of September, but its share of the emerging East Asian total remained small. The aggregate LCY bonds outstanding of ASEAN markets comprised 9.5% of the total emerging East Asian LCY bond market at the end of September (**Figure 3**). The LCY bond market in the PRC (USD21.3 trillion) comprised nearly 80% of the regional total at the end of September,

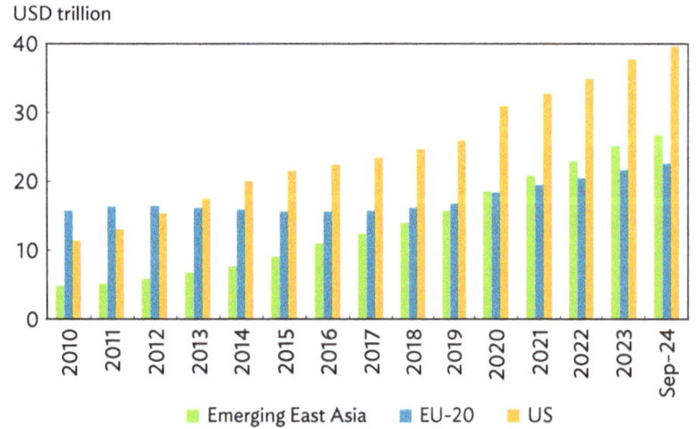

Figure 1: Local Currency Bonds Outstanding in Emerging East Asia, the European Union 20, and the United States

EU-20 = European Union 20, US = United States, USD = United States dollar.

Notes:
1. Emerging East Asia is defined to include the Association of Southeast Asian Nations plus the People's Republic of China; Hong Kong, China; and the Republic of Korea.
2. The EU-20 includes the member markets of Austria, Belgium, Croatia, Cyprus, Estonia, Finland, France, Germany, Greece, Ireland, Italy, Latvia, Lithuania, Luxembourg, Malta, the Netherlands, Portugal, Slovakia, Slovenia, and Spain.

Sources: People's Republic of China (CEIC Data Company); Hong Kong, China (Hong Kong Monetary Authority); EU-20 (European Central Bank); Indonesia (Bank Indonesia; Directorate General of Budget Financing and Risk Management, Ministry of Finance; and Indonesia Stock Exchange); Republic of Korea (Bank of Korea and KG Zeroin Corporation); Malaysia (Bank Negara Malaysia); Philippines (Bangko Sentral ng Pilipinas, Bureau of the Treasury, and Bloomberg LP); Singapore (Monetary Authority of Singapore and Bloomberg LP); Thailand (Bank of Thailand); United States (Securities Industry and Financial Markets Association and Bloomberg LP); and Viet Nam (Hanoi Stock Exchange, State Bank of Vietnam, Vietnam Bond Market Association, and Bloomberg LP).

---

[4] Emerging East Asia is defined to include member states of the Association of Southeast Asian Nations plus the People's Republic of China; Hong Kong, China; and the Republic of Korea.

Table 1: Size and Composition of Select Emerging East Asian Local Currency Bond Markets

	Q3 2023		Q2 2024		Q3 2024			Growth Rate (%) Q3 2024	
	Amount (USD billion)	% of GDP	Amount (USD billion)	% of GDP	Amount (USD billion)	% share	% of GDP	q-o-q	y-o-y
People's Republic of China									
Total	18,879	110.5	19,971	113.0	21,326	100.0	115.4	3.1	8.6
Treasury and Other Government	12,051	70.5	13,320	75.3	14,366	67.4	77.7	4.2	14.6
Central Bank	2	0.01	2	0.01	2	0.01	0.01	(1.7)	(1.7)
Corporate	6,826	39.9	6,649	37.6	6,958	32.6	37.6	1.1	(2.0)
Hong Kong, China									
Total	386	103.4	389	98.4	384	100.0	95.3	(1.7)	(1.2)
Treasury and Other Government	37	9.9	33	8.4	29	7.4	7.1	(14.2)	(23.1)
Government	158	42.5	164	41.6	167	43.4	41.4	1.0	4.4
Corporate	190	51.0	191	48.4	189	49.2	46.8	(1.8)	(1.6)
Indonesia									
Total	403	30.1	440	33.6	498	100.0	34.7	4.8	21.0
Treasury and Other Government	366	27.3	364	27.9	403	80.9	28.0	2.3	7.8
Central Bank	8	0.6	47	3.6	65	13.1	4.5	28	665.8
Corporate	29	2.1	28	2.2	30	6.0	2.1	(1.7)	2.7
Republic of Korea									
Total	2,347	133.7	2,392	132.5	2,504	100.0	138.7	0.01	4.0
Treasury and Other Government	893	50.9	911	50.4	954	38.1	52.8	0.02	4.1
Central Bank	93	5.3	87	4.8	87	3.5	2.1	(4.8)	(9.3)
Corporate	1,361	77.5	1,394	77.2	1,464	58.5	81.1	0.3	4.8
Malaysia									
Total	422	127.4	437	128.2	504	100.0	127.6	0.9	4.8
Treasury and Other Government	240	72.4	254	74.6	294	58.4	74.5	1.2	7.6
Central Bank	3	1.0	0.4	0.1	0	0.0	0.0	(100.0)	(100.0)
Corporate	179	54.0	182	53.5	210	41.6	53.1	0.6	2.9
Philippines									
Total	210	50.2	214	49.3	232	100.0	50.2	3.8	9.3
Treasury and Other Government	171	40.8	178	41.0	193	83.0	41.7	3.6	11.7
Central Bank	12	2.9	14	3.2	16	6.8	3.4	8.5	30.7
Corporate	27	6.5	22	5.0	24	10.2	5.1	3.1	(14.9)
Singapore									
Total	535	109.3	606	117.7	651	100.0	126.4	1.8	14.4
Treasury and Other Government	196	39.9	222	43.2	236	36.3	45.8	0.6	13.5
Central Bank	204	41.7	238	46.1	262	40.2	50.8	4.4	20.5
Corporate	135	27.7	146	28.4	153	23.5	29.8	(0.7)	6.4
Thailand									
Total	455	92.9	460	92.8	531	100.0	93.0	1.1	3.2
Treasury and Other Government	256	52.3	269	54.3	312	58.7	54.6	1.5	7.6
Central Bank	67	13.7	61	12.3	73	13.8	12.8	5.4	(3.9)
Corporate	132	26.9	130	26.3	146	27.5	25.6	(1.8)	(1.9)
Viet Nam									
Total	108	26.4	115	27.2	123	100.0	27.3	3.1	14.1
Treasury and Other Government	77	18.8	81	19.2	88	72.1	19.7	5.3	15.9
Central Bank	4	0.9	6	1.4	3	2.3	0.6	(52.6)	(24.7)
Corporate	28	6.7	28	6.6	31	25.5	7.0	8.4	14.8
Emerging East Asia									
Total	23,746	104.6	25,022	107.0	26,753	100.0	109.1	2.7	8.2
Treasury and Other Government	14,286	62.9	15,632	66.8	16,874	63.1	68.8	3.7	13.4
Central Bank	552	2.4	619	2.6	674	2.5	2.7	3.7	16.5
Corporate	8,907	39.2	8,771	37.5	9,205	34.4	37.5	0.8	(0.7)
Japan									
Total	9,034	230.4	8,559	229.6	9,636	100.0	229.2	0.5	2.6
Treasury and Other Government	8,339	212.7	7,889	211.7	8,876	92.1	211.1	0.4	2.3
Central Bank	13	0.3	23	0.6	25	0.3	0.6	(2.4)	84.8
Corporate	682	17.4	647	17.4	736	7.6	17.5	1.6	3.7

( ) = negative, GDP = gross domestic product, q-o-q = quarter-on-quarter, Q2 = second quarter, Q3 = third quarter, USD = United States dollar, y-o-y = year-on-year.

Notes:
1. For Singapore, corporate bonds outstanding are based on *AsianBondsOnline* estimates.
2. GDP data are from CEIC Data Company. Q3 2024 GDP data are carried over from Q2 2024 for the Republic of Korea and Singapore.
3. Bloomberg LP end-of-period local currency–USD rates are used.
4. Growth rates are calculated from a local currency base and do not include currency effects. For emerging East Asia, growth figures are based on 30 September 2024 currency exchange rates and do not include currency effects.

Sources: People's Republic of China (CEIC Data Company); Hong Kong, China (Hong Kong Monetary Authority); Indonesia (Bank Indonesia; Directorate General of Budget Financing and Risk Management, Ministry of Finance; and Indonesia Stock Exchange); Japan (Japan Securities Dealers Association); Republic of Korea (Bank of Korea and KG Zeroin Corporation); Malaysia (Bank Negara Malaysia); Philippines (Bangko Sentral ng Pilipinas, Bureau of the Treasury, and Bloomberg LP); Singapore (Monetary Authority of Singapore and Bloomberg LP); Thailand (Bank of Thailand); and Viet Nam (Hanoi Stock Exchange, State Bank of Vietnam, Vietnam Bond Market Association, and Bloomberg LP).

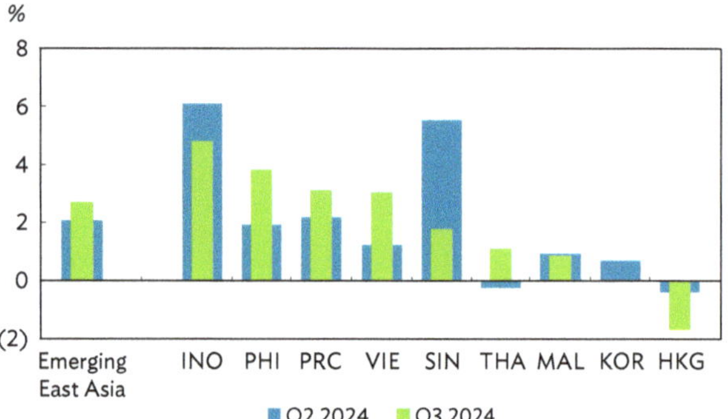

Figure 2: Growth of Select Emerging East Asian Local Currency Bond Markets (q-o-q, %)

( ) = negative; HKG = Hong Kong, China; INO = Indonesia; KOR = Republic of Korea; MAL = Malaysia; PHI = Philippines; PRC = People's Republic of China; Q2 = second quarter; Q3 = third quarter; q-o-q = quarter-on-quarter; SIN = Singapore; THA = Thailand; VIE = Viet Nam.

Notes:
1. For Singapore, corporate bonds outstanding are based on *AsianBondsOnline* estimates.
2. Growth rates are calculated from a local currency base and do not include currency effects. For emerging East Asia, growth figures are based on 30 September 2024 currency exchange rates and do not include currency effects.
3. Growth rate for the Republic of Korea for Q3 2024 was 0.01% q-o-q.
4. Emerging East Asia is defined to include member states of the Association of Southeast Asian Nations plus the People's Republic of China; Hong Kong, China; and the Republic of Korea.

Sources: People's Republic of China (CEIC Data Company); Hong Kong, China (Hong Kong Monetary Authority); Indonesia (Bank Indonesia; Directorate General of Budget Financing and Risk Management, Ministry of Finance; and Indonesia Stock Exchange); Republic of Korea (Bank of Korea and KG Zeroin Corporation); Malaysia (Bank Negara Malaysia); Philippines (Bangko Sentral ng Pilipinas, Bureau of the Treasury, and Bloomberg LP); Singapore (Monetary Authority of Singapore and Bloomberg LP); Thailand (Bank of Thailand); and Viet Nam (Hanoi Stock Exchange, State Bank of Vietnam, Vietnam Bond Market Association, and Bloomberg LP).

Figure 3: Local Currency Bonds Outstanding in Emerging East Asia by Economy and Type of Bond as of 30 September 2024

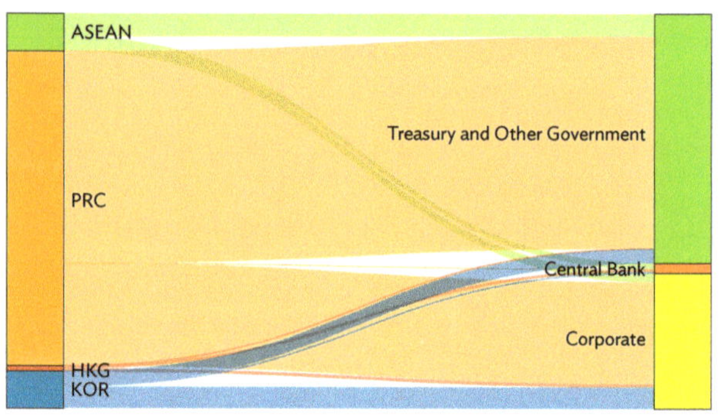

ASEAN = Association of Southeast Asian Nations; HKG = Hong Kong, China; KOR = Republic of Korea; PRC = People's Republic of China.

Note: ASEAN comprises the markets of Indonesia, Malaysia, the Philippines, Singapore, Thailand, and Viet Nam.

Source: *AsianBondsOnline* calculations based on various local sources.

Figure 4: Maturity Structure of Local Currency Treasury Bonds Outstanding in Select Emerging East Asian Markets as of 30 September 2024

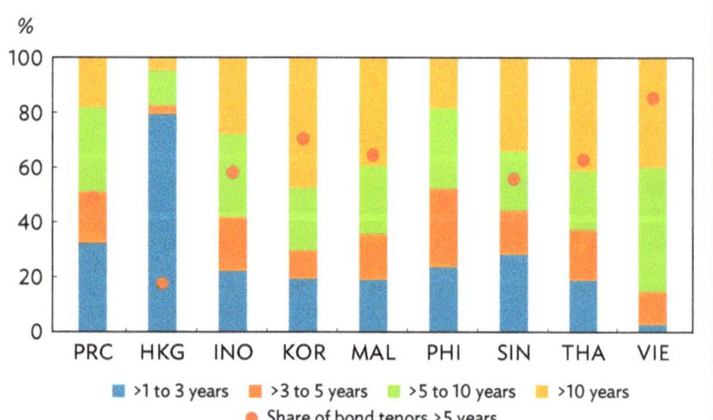

HKG = Hong Kong, China; INO = Indonesia; KOR = Republic of Korea; MAL = Malaysia; PHI = Philippines; PRC = People's Republic of China; SIN = Singapore; THA = Thailand; VIE = Viet Nam.

Note: Treasury bonds are local-currency-denominated, fixed-income securities issued by a government with maturities longer than 1 year.

Sources: People's Republic of China (Bloomberg LP); Hong Kong, China (Hong Kong Monetary Authority); Indonesia (Directorate General of Budget Financing and Risk Management, Ministry of Finance); Republic of Korea (Bloomberg LP); Malaysia (Bank Negara Malaysia Fully Automated System for Issuing/Tendering); Philippines (Bureau of the Treasury); Singapore (Monetary Authority of Singapore); Thailand (Bank of Thailand); and Viet Nam (Hanoi Stock Exchange).

while that of the Republic of Korea (USD2.5 trillion) and Hong Kong, China (USD0.4 trillion) accounted for the remaining 9.4% and 1.4%, respectively. Treasury bonds (USD16.9 trillion) continued to comprise most of the region's LCY bond market, accounting for 63.1% of total LCY bonds outstanding at the end of September. Corporate bonds (USD9.2 trillion) and central bank bonds (USD0.7 trillion) represented the remaining 34.4% and 2.5% shares, respectively.

The maturity structure of most emerging East Asian Treasury bond markets favors medium- to long-term financing, providing governments with longer repayment periods. Securities with remaining maturities longer than 5 years accounted for 54.0% of emerging East Asian Treasury bonds outstanding at the end of September (**Figure 4**). ASEAN markets had an even higher share (60.6%) of Treasury bonds outstanding with remaining tenors of more than 5 years. The size-weighted average tenor of Treasury bonds outstanding in emerging East Asia at the end of September was 9.0 years, slightly longer than the corresponding average tenors of Treasury bonds outstanding in the EU-20 (8.6 years) and the US (8.2 years). At the end of September, the size-weighted average tenor of Treasury bonds outstanding in ASEAN was 9.0 years, while those in the PRC and the Republic of Korea were 8.2 years and 12.5 years, respectively. Meanwhile, the size-weighted average tenor of Treasury bonds outstanding in Hong Kong, China stood at only 2.7 years, as around 83.1% of outstanding Hong Kong Special Administrative Region government bonds and inflation-linked securities had remaining maturities of less than 3 years.

Institutional investors remained the largest bondholders in emerging East Asia in Q3 2024, accounting for a combined share of 64.2% of Treasury bonds. Investor ownership of Treasury bonds in the region remained concentrated among banks and insurance and pension funds, with average regional holding shares of 35.5% and 28.7%, respectively (**Figure 5**). However, there still was some variation among regional members. Banks were the largest holder in the PRC (68.1%) and in the Philippines (45.7%). On the other hand, insurance and pension funds had the most substantial holdings of Treasury bonds in

Viet Nam (59.8%), Thailand (43.1%), Malaysia (35.1%), and the Republic of Korea (29.0%). Variations in central bank holdings across the region were also noted, with Indonesia recording the highest share at 25.0%, while central bank holdings in all other emerging East Asian markets comprised about 6.2% or less. Central bank investments in government bond markets are mostly utilized for open market operations. However, in Indonesia, they are also undertaken as part of the central bank's efforts to support the bond market. Meanwhile, foreign investor participation remained strong in Malaysia and the Republic of Korea with shareholdings of 21.4% and 18.5%, respectively. At the end of Q3 2024, Viet Nam and the PRC scored the highest in the Herfindahl-Hirschman Index, a trend similar to past quarters, indicating a less diverse investor structure in both markets.[5] Indonesia and the Republic of Korea are the region's most diversified markets in terms of investor profile, as Treasury bond ownership is broadly spread out among varied investor groups in both economies.

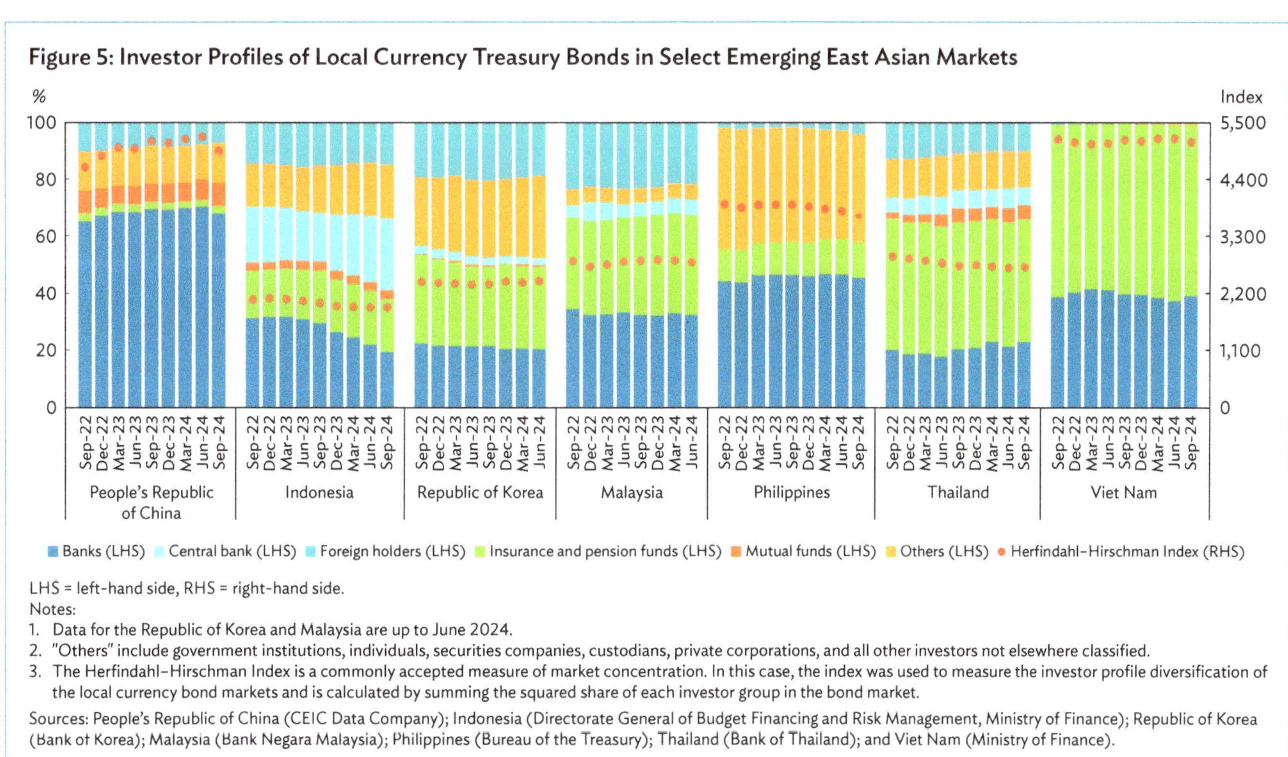

Figure 5: Investor Profiles of Local Currency Treasury Bonds in Select Emerging East Asian Markets

LHS = left-hand side, RHS = right-hand side.
Notes:
1.   Data for the Republic of Korea and Malaysia are up to June 2024.
2.   "Others" include government institutions, individuals, securities companies, custodians, private corporations, and all other investors not elsewhere classified.
3.   The Herfindahl–Hirschman Index is a commonly accepted measure of market concentration. In this case, the index was used to measure the investor profile diversification of the local currency bond markets and is calculated by summing the squared share of each investor group in the bond market.

Sources: People's Republic of China (CEIC Data Company); Indonesia (Directorate General of Budget Financing and Risk Management, Ministry of Finance); Republic of Korea (Bank of Korea); Malaysia (Bank Negara Malaysia); Philippines (Bureau of the Treasury); Thailand (Bank of Thailand); and Viet Nam (Ministry of Finance).

---

[5]   The Herfindahl-Hirschman Index is a commonly accepted measure of market concentration. The index is used to measure the investor profile diversification of the region's local currency bond markets and is calculated by summing the squared share of each investor group in the bond market.

Section 2. Local Currency Bond Issuance

LCY bond issuance in emerging East Asia rose 11.3% q-o-q in Q3 2024, supported by growth in both the government and corporate bond segments. Total issuance reached USD3.0 trillion in Q3 2024, nearly 70.0% of the issuance in the US (USD4.3 trillion) and almost four times that in the EU-20 (USD0.8 trillion). Government bonds comprised 45.1% of the total bond issuance in Q3 2024, with growth in this segment largely driven by the PRC (**Figure 6**). The Government of the PRC continued to step up its fiscal policy support to aid the economy via increased issuance of local government bonds and another batch of its ultra long-term special Treasury bonds. Meanwhile, corporate bonds accounted for nearly a third of total issuance and grew at a faster pace during the quarter. Issuance in the PRC surged in Q3 2024 due to low bond yields and as banks continued to raise funds to meet regulatory capital requirements. In the Republic of Korea and most of ASEAN, corporate bond issuance rebounded as companies took advantage of declining bond yields on improved market conditions amid the expected rate cuts by the Federal Reserve, the Bank of Korea, and some ASEAN central banks.

Government bond issuance rose 20.1% q-o-q to USD1.3 trillion in Q3 2024, driven by the surge in issuance in the PRC. The PRC continued to be the largest issuer of government bonds in the region with an 88.5% share of the regional total (**Figure 7**). Issuance in the PRC surged 24.5% q-o-q as the government continued to raise funds to support its various economic stimulus measures amid weak economic growth. Issuance of local government bonds and Treasury bonds posted large increases of 66.5% q-o-q and 15.4% q-o-q, respectively, in Q3 2024. Meanwhile, total issuance of government bonds in ASEAN markets, which collectively accounted for 8.2% of the regional total, marginally fell by 0.9% q-o-q as higher issuance volumes in Indonesia (26.3% q-o-q), the Philippines (34.0% q-o-q), and Viet Nam (51.0% q-o-q) were offset by contractions in the other markets. Issuance of government bonds in these markets increased as market conditions improved, including the policy easing measures conducted by their respective central banks during the quarter. Meanwhile, issuance in the Republic of Korea and the remaining ASEAN markets contracted as their governments frontloaded their borrowing in the first half of the year. Issuance of central bank bonds in the region marginally fell by 0.5% q-o-q in Q3 2024.

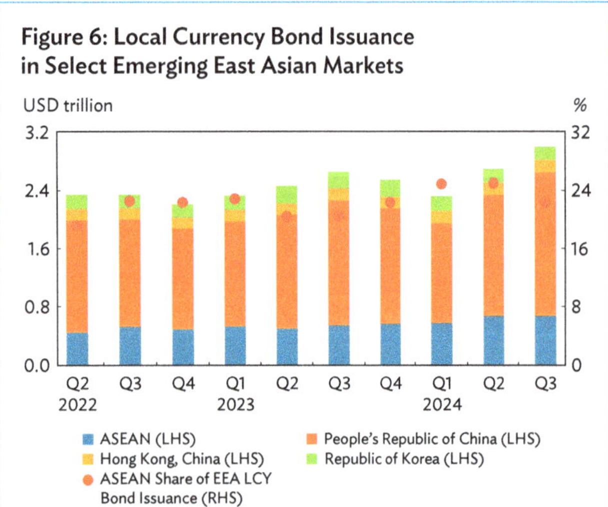

Figure 6: Local Currency Bond Issuance in Select Emerging East Asian Markets

ASEAN = Association of Southeast Asian Nations, EEA = emerging East Asia, LCY = local currency, LHS = left-hand side, Q1 = first quarter, Q2 = second quarter, Q3 = third quarter, Q4 = fourth quarter, RHS = right-hand side, USD = United States dollar.

Notes:
1. ASEAN comprises the markets of Indonesia, Malaysia, the Philippines, Singapore, Thailand, and Viet Nam.
2. Figures were computed based on 30 September 2024 currency exchange rates and do not include currency effects.

Source: People's Republic of China (CEIC Data Company); Hong Kong, China (Hong Kong Monetary Authority); Indonesia (Bank Indonesia; Directorate General of Budget Financing and Risk Management, Ministry of Finance; and Indonesia Stock Exchange); Republic of Korea (Bank of Korea and KG Zeroin Corporation); Malaysia (Bank Negara Malaysia); Philippines (Bangko Sentral ng Pilipinas, Bureau of the Treasury, and Bloomberg LP); Singapore (Monetary Authority of Singapore and Bloomberg LP); Thailand (Bank of Thailand and Thai Bond Market Association); and Viet Nam (Hanoi Stock Exchange, State Bank of Vietnam, Vietnam Bond Market Association, and Bloomberg LP).

Figure 7: Local Currency Bond Issuance in Emerging East Asia by Economy and Type of Bond in the Third Quarter of 2024

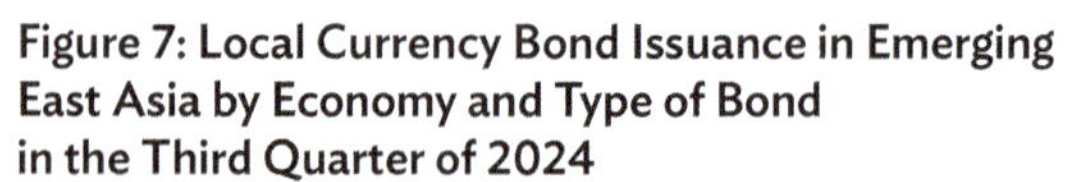
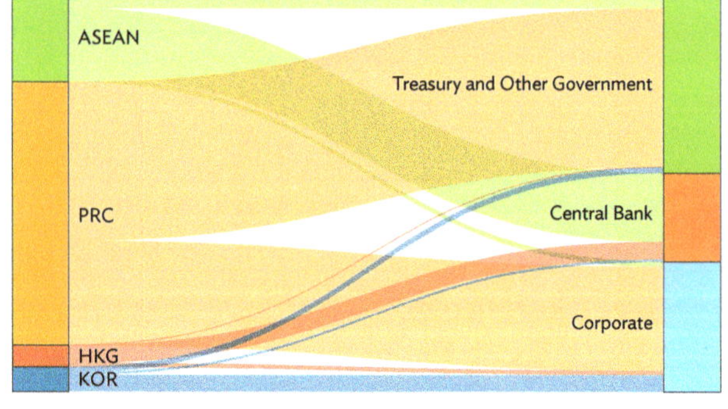

ASEAN = Association of Southeast Asian Nations; HKG = Hong Kong, China; KOR = Republic of Korea; PRC = People's Republic of China.

Note: ASEAN comprises the markets of Indonesia, Malaysia, the Philippines, Singapore, Thailand, and Viet Nam.

Source: *AsianBondsOnline* calculations based on various local sources.

Corporate bond issuance posted rapid growth of 9.1% q-o-q to reach USD975.8 billion in Q3 2024, amid a low-interest rate environment. Corporate bond issuance growth in the PRC accelerated to 10.4% q-o-q during the quarter from 9.2% q-o-q in Q2 2024, driven by growth in credit bonds. Credit bonds issued by nonfinancial companies rose 12.8% q-o-q as companies took advantage of low yields and the PBOC cut key policy rates to support economic activities. Corporate bond issuance in the Republic of Korea and in ASEAN markets also rose 7.4% q-o-q and 3.3% q-o-q, respectively, on improved market conditions amid increased expectations the Federal Reserve, the Bank of Korea, and some ASEAN central banks would cut policy rates (**Table 2**).

Treasury bond issuance in the region continued to carry medium- to long-term tenors in Q3 2024. Bonds with tenors of more than 5 years comprised 61.1% of the total issuance in emerging East Asia and 70.0% in ASEAN markets during Q3 2024 (**Figure 8a**). Viet Nam and Malaysia had the highest shares in Q3 2024 at 97.0% and 90.5%, respectively (**Figure 8b**). The resulting size-weighted average maturity of Treasury bond issuance was 10.0 years for emerging East Asia, with ASEAN economies having a slightly higher average of 10.3 years versus non-ASEAN economies' average of 10.0 years.

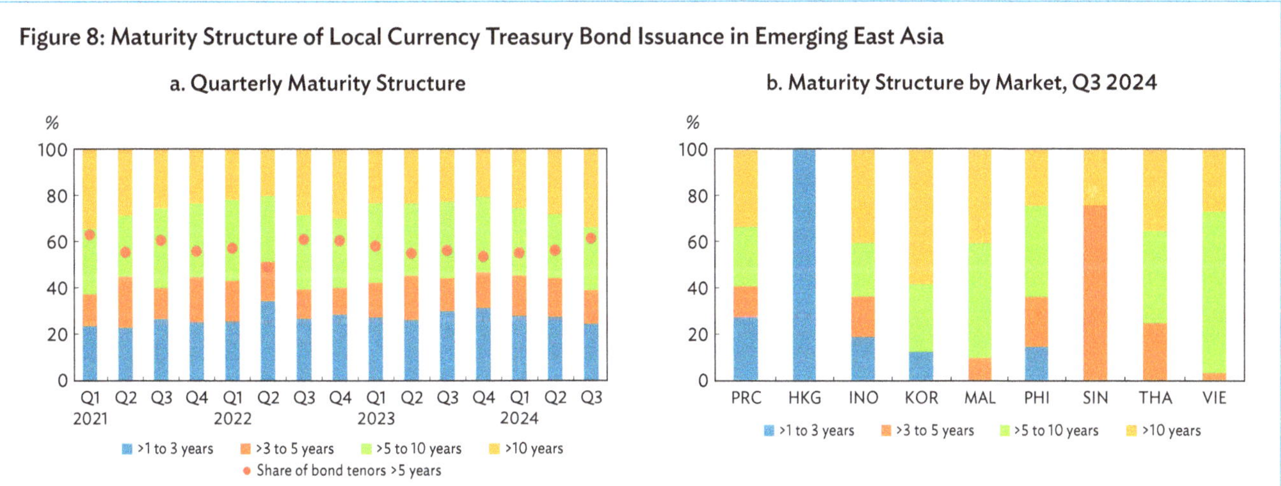

Figure 8: Maturity Structure of Local Currency Treasury Bond Issuance in Emerging East Asia

HKG = Hong Kong, China; INO = Indonesia; KOR = Republic of Korea; MAL = Malaysia; PHI = Philippines; PRC = People's Republic of China; Q1 = first quarter; Q2 = second quarter; Q3 = third quarter; Q4 = fourth quarter; SIN = Singapore; THA = Thailand; VIE = Viet Nam.

Notes:
1. Figures were computed based on 30 September 2024 currency exchange rates and do not include currency effects.
2. Treasury bonds are local-currency-denominated, fixed-income securities issued by a government with maturities longer than 1 year.

Source: *AsianBondsOnline* calculations based on various local sources.

Table 2: Local-Currency-Denominated Bond Issuance

	Q3 2023		Q2 2024		Q3 2024		Growth Rate (%)	
	Amount (USD billion)	% share	Amount (USD billion)	% share	Amount (USD billion)	% share	Q3 2024 q-o-q	Q3 2024 y-o-y
People's Republic of China								
Total	1,650	100.0	1,609	100.0	1,974	100.0	18.5	15.1
Treasury and Other Government	960	58.2	923	57.4	1,190	60.3	24.5	19.2
Central Bank	0	0.0	0	0.0	0	0.0	–	–
Corporate	689	41.8	686	42.6	784	39.7	10.4	9.4
Hong Kong, China								
Total	168	100.0	163	100.0	164	100.0	(0.1)	(3.3)
Treasury and Other Government	7	4.4	0.2	0.1	0.2	0.1	0.0	(97.4)
Government	127	75.6	130	79.8	133	81.2	1.7	4.0
Corporate	34	20.0	33	20.1	31	18.7	(7.4)	(9.8)
Indonesia								
Total	31	100.0	46	100.0	51	100.0	1.9	62.3
Treasury and Other Government	13	40.7	12	25.7	16	31.8	26.3	26.8
Central Bank	16	50.2	32	69.8	33	64.2	(6.2)	107.4
Corporate	3	9.1	2	4.5	2	4.0	(9.8)	(27.9)
Republic of Korea								
Total	215	100.0	176	100.0	184	100.0	(0.3)	(16.8)
Treasury and Other Government	47	21.7	49	27.8	43	23.5	(15.6)	(10.0)
Central Bank	25	11.7	16	9.1	16	8.5	(6.9)	(39.7)
Corporate	143	66.5	111	63.1	125	68.0	7.4	(15.0)
Malaysia								
Total	37	100.0	25	100.0	26	100.0	(9.6)	(40.3)
Treasury and Other Government	12	32.6	13	53.7	14	52.9	(10.9)	(3.1)
Central Bank	16	42.3	3	10.3	0	0.0	(100.0)	(100.0)
Corporate	9	25.0	9	36.0	12	47.1	18.2	12.3
Philippines								
Total	42	100.0	45	100.0	52	100.0	11.0	22.8
Treasury and Other Government	10	24.6	10	22.9	14	27.6	34.0	37.8
Central Bank	31	73.7	34	75.5	35	66.7	(1.9)	11.1
Corporate	1	1.7	1	1.6	3	5.7	283.9	318.0
Singapore								
Total	324	100.0	417	100.0	424	100.0	(3.7)	23.1
Treasury and Other Government	35	10.8	46	11.1	41	9.7	(15.6)	10.2
Central Bank	288	88.9	368	88.1	380	89.6	(2.1)	24.1
Corporate	1	0.3	3	0.8	3	0.7	(22.4)	171.7
Thailand								
Total	61	100.0	62	100.0	69	100.0	(2.6)	(1.2)
Treasury and Other Government	15	24.0	18	29.9	21	30.1	(1.8)	24.1
Central Bank	33	54.0	30	48.1	35	51.8	4.7	(5.4)
Corporate	13	22.0	14	22.0	12	18.1	(19.8)	(18.7)
Viet Nam								
Total	9	100.0	29	100.0	40	100.0	35.0	347.1
Treasury and Other Government	3	33.5	3	10.4	5	11.6	51.0	54.7
Central Bank	4	42.2	23	79.4	31	77.9	32.4	724.1
Corporate	2	24.2	3	10.2	4	10.5	39.3	94.3
Emerging East Asia								
Total	2,538	100.0	2,572	100.0	2,983	100.0	11.3	12.8
Treasury and Other Government	1,103	43.4	1,075	41.8	1,344	45.1	20.1	17.1
Central Bank	540	21.3	636	24.7	663	22.2	(0.5)	17.1
Corporate	896	35.3	861	33.5	976	32.7	9.1	4.9
Japan								
Total	378	100.0	330	100.0	379	100.0	2.5	(3.6)
Treasury and Other Government	340	89.9	296	89.8	343	90.4	3.3	(3.0)
Central Bank	0	0.0	0	0.0	0	0.0	–	–
Corporate	38	10.1	34	10.2	36	9.6	(4.4)	(8.7)

( ) = negative, – = not applicable, Q2 = second quarter, Q3 = third quarter, q-o-q = quarter-on-quarter, USD = United States dollar, y-o-y = year-on-year.

Notes:
1. Data reflect gross bond issuance.
2. Bloomberg LP end-of-period local currency–USD rates are used.
3. Growth rates are calculated from a local currency base and do not include currency effects. For emerging East Asia, growth figures are based on 30 September 2024 currency exchange rates and do not include currency effects.

Source: People's Republic of China (CEIC Data Company); Hong Kong, China (Hong Kong Monetary Authority); Indonesia (Bank Indonesia, Directorate General of Budget Financing and Risk Management, Ministry of Finance; and Indonesia Stock Exchange); Japan (Japan Securities Dealers Association); Republic of Korea (Bank of Korea and KG Zeroin Corporation); Malaysia (Bank Negara Malaysia); Philippines (Bangko Sentral ng Pilipinas, Bureau of the Treasury, and Bloomberg LP); Singapore (Monetary Authority of Singapore and Bloomberg LP); Thailand (Bank of Thailand and Thai Bond Market Association); and Viet Nam (Hanoi Stock Exchange, State Bank of Vietnam, Vietnam Bond Market Association, and Bloomberg LP).

Section 3. Intra-Regional Bond Issuance

Emerging East Asian intra-regional bond issuance contracted 5.8% q-o-q in Q3 2024 to USD11.0 billion.[6] Decreased intra-regional bond issuance during the quarter was driven by reduced debt sales from Hong Kong, China and the Republic of Korea, outweighing increased issuance from Singapore, Malaysia, and the PRC (**Figure 9**). Hong Kong, China, whose total issuance declined 7.0% q-o-q to USD9.8 billion in Q3 2024, remained the top issuer of intra-regional bonds during the quarter, comprising 89.4% of the regional total. In July, the Government of the Hong Kong Special Administrative Region of the People's Republic of China issued USD1.4 billion worth of CNY-denominated green bonds with tenors ranging from 2 years to 30 years. In addition, China Merchants Group—a state-owned logistics firm based in Hong Kong, China—also issued an aggregate USD1.4 billion worth of CNY-denominated bonds, making them the top two issuers of intra-regional bonds during

the quarter, with aggregate issuance equivalent to 26.0% of the intra-regional issuance total. Meanwhile, the Republic of Korea's total intra-regional issuance declined by 53.2% q-o-q in Q3 2024 to USD0.2 billion, accounting for 2.0% of the emerging East Asian total.

The region's intra-regional bond issuance during the quarter was dominated by the financial sector and CNY-denominated instruments. Intra-regional CNY-denominated issuance totaled USD10.6 billion in Q3 2024, accounting for 96.8% of emerging East Asia's intra-regional total, while issuances denominated in Hong Kong dollars, Singapore dollars, and Indonesian rupiah collectively accounted for only 3.2% (**Figure 10**). By sector, the finance industry was the largest issuer of intra-regional bonds during the quarter with aggregate issuance of USD2.5 billion, comprising 22.8% of the region's total. This was followed by the transportation sector (USD2.4 billion) with a 21.5% share of the market.

Figure 9: Intra-Regional Bond Issuance in Select Emerging East Asian Economies

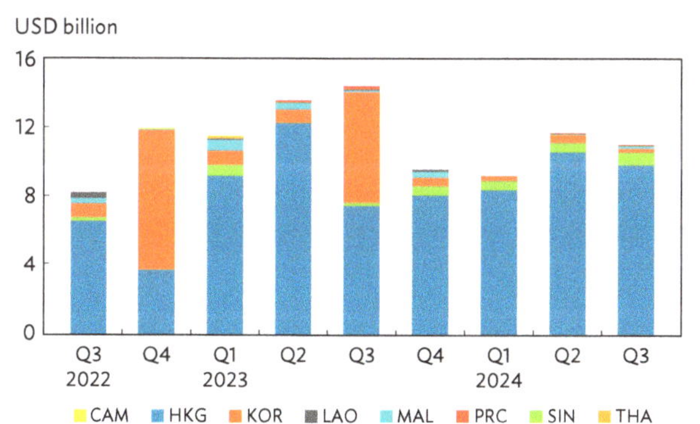

CAM = Cambodia; HKG = Hong Kong, China; KOR = Republic of Korea; LAO = Lao People's Democratic Republic; MAL = Malaysia; PRC = People's Republic of China; Q1 = first quarter; Q2 = second quarter; Q3 = third quarter; Q4 = fourth quarter; SIN = Singapore; THA = Thailand; USD = United States dollar.

Notes:
1. Emerging East Asia is defined to include member states of the Association of Southeast Asian Nations plus the People's Republic of China; Hong Kong, China; and the Republic of Korea.
2. Intra-regional bond issuance is defined as emerging East Asian bond issuance denominated in a regional currency excluding the issuer's home currency.
3. Figures were computed based on 30 September 2024 currency exchange rates and do not include currency effects.

Source: *AsianBondsOnline* calculations based on Bloomberg LP data.

Figure 10: Intra-Regional Bond Issuance in Emerging East Asia by Economy, Currency, and Sector in the Third Quarter of 2024

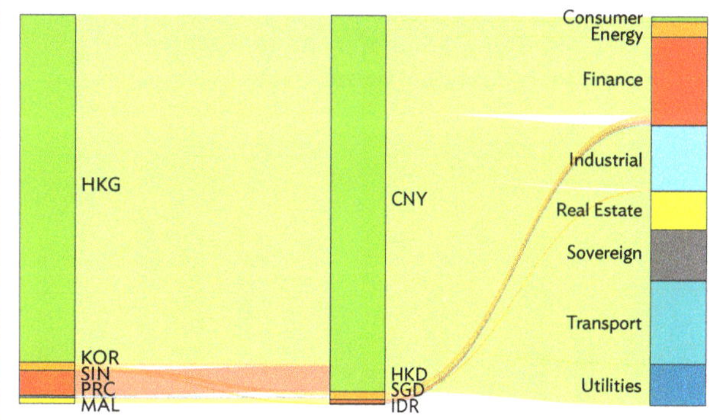

CNY = Chinese yuan; HKD = Hong Kong dollar; HKG = Hong Kong, China; IDR = Indonesian rupiah; KOR = Republic of Korea; MAL = Malaysia; PRC = People's Republic of China; SGD = Singapore dollar; SIN = Singapore.

Note: Intra-regional bond issuance is defined as emerging East Asian bond issuance denominated in a regional currency excluding the issuer's home currency.

Source: *AsianBondsOnline* calculations based on Bloomberg LP data.

---

[6] Intra-regional bond issuance is defined as emerging East Asian bond issuance denominated in a regional currency, excluding the issuer's home currency.

Section 4. G3 Currency Bond Issuance

Emerging East Asian G3 currency bond issuance rose to USD68.6 billion in Q3 2024, reflecting growth of 9.1% q-o-q and 65.2% y-o-y (Figure 11).[7] Declining interest rates encouraged the issuance of G3 currency bonds amid expectations of easing monetary stances by the Federal Reserve and the European Central Bank. Much of the issuance during the quarter came from the PRC, which accounted for over 38.0% of all G3 currency bond issuance in the region, despite a 4.0% q-o-q decline to USD26.5 billion (**Figure 12**). ASEAN economies' G3 bond issuance of USD21.6 billion accounted for 31.5% of the emerging East Asian total. ASEAN issuance rose 24.3% q-o-q, buoyed by issuances from Indonesia, as its central bank sold foreign currency instruments in the form of Sekuritas Valas Bank Indonesia. Additionally, in the Philippines, the issuance of government-issued sustainable bonds and securities from the San Miguel Global Power Corporation significantly contributed to the overall increase in ASEAN issuance. Among ASEAN markets, the top issuer of G3 currency bonds during the quarter was Bank Indonesia as it continued to issue foreign currency securities to stabilize the rupiah

Figure 12: G3 Currency Bond Issuance
in Emerging East Asia in the Third Quarter of 2024

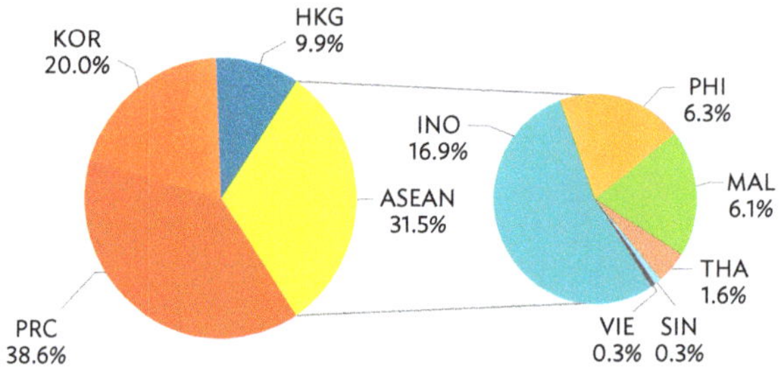

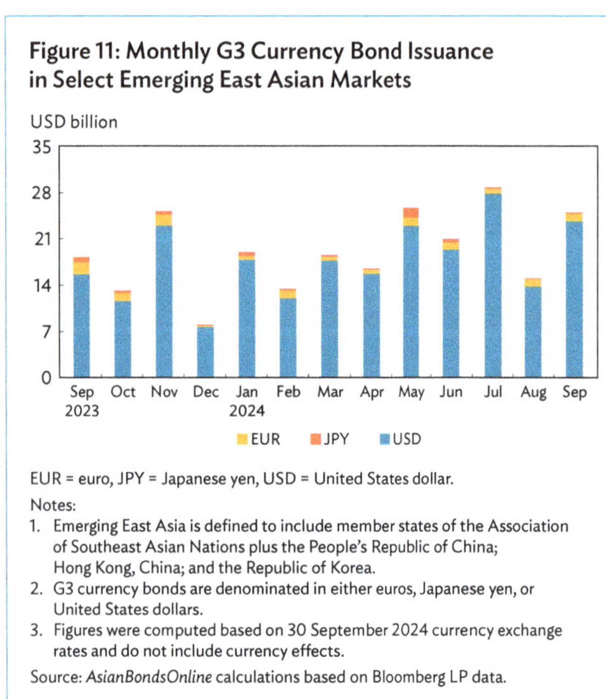

ASEAN = Association of Southeast Asian Nations; HKG = Hong Kong, China; INO = Indonesia; KOR = Republic of Korea; MAL = Malaysia; PHI = Philippines; PRC = People's Republic of China; SIN = Singapore; THA = Thailand; VIE = Viet Nam.
Notes:
1. Emerging East Asia is defined to include member states of ASEAN plus the People's Republic of China; Hong Kong, China; and the Republic of Korea.
2. G3 currency bonds are denominated in either euros, Japanese yen, or United States dollars.
Source: *AsianBondsOnline* calculations based on Bloomberg LP data.

exchange rate and support development of the money market. The next largest issuers were the Government of Indonesia and the Government of the Philippines as part of their respective foreign currency borrowing plans to support their budget deficits. During the quarter, the Government of the Hong Kong Special Administrative Region of the People's Republic of China also issued USD- and EUR-denominated green bonds under its Government Sustainable Bond Programme to promote low-carbon emissions and solidify Hong Kong, China's position as a sustainable finance hub.

Section 5. Yield Curve Movements

In emerging East Asia, six out of nine markets saw their yield curves steepen between 2 September and 31 October, as indicated by a rise in the 10-year and 2-year yield spread, on uncertainties regarding the path of monetary policy by the Federal Reserve and the outcome of the US elections (Figure 13, a and b). The PRC saw its 10-year versus 2-year yield spread steepen largely over domestic issues as recent stimulus measures are expected to worsen the fiscal deficit. All other markets that had their 10-year and 2-year yield spreads widen did so largely on the back of uncertainties

Figure 11: Monthly G3 Currency Bond Issuance
in Select Emerging East Asian Markets

USD billion

EUR = euro, JPY = Japanese yen, USD = United States dollar.
Notes:
1. Emerging East Asia is defined to include member states of the Association of Southeast Asian Nations plus the People's Republic of China; Hong Kong, China; and the Republic of Korea.
2. G3 currency bonds are denominated in either euros, Japanese yen, or United States dollars.
3. Figures were computed based on 30 September 2024 currency exchange rates and do not include currency effects.
Source: *AsianBondsOnline* calculations based on Bloomberg LP data.

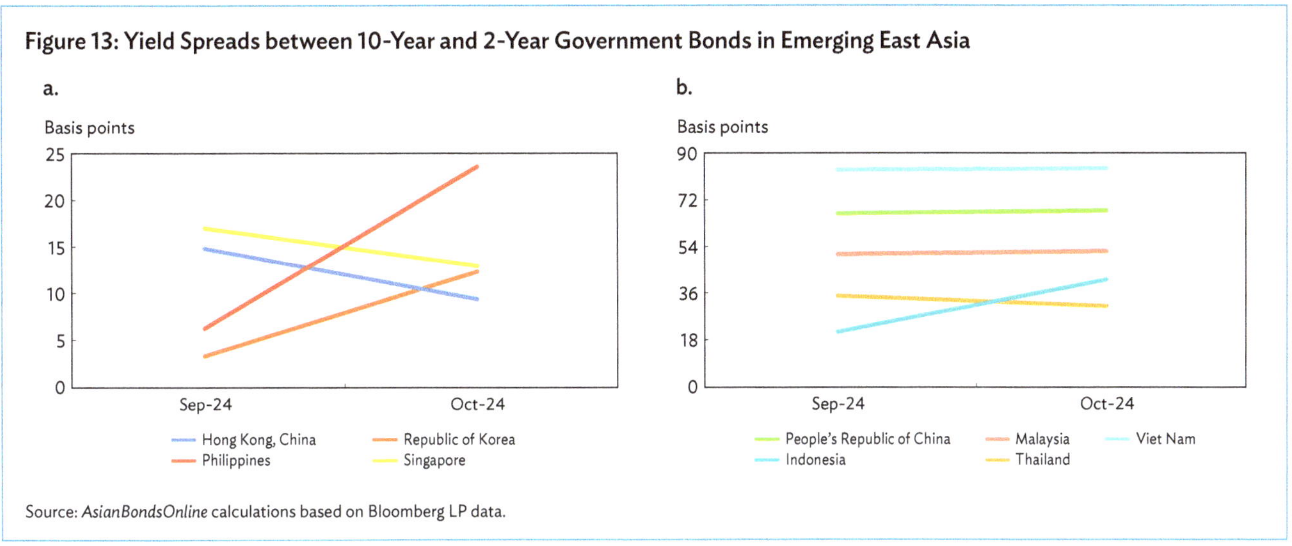

Figure 13: Yield Spreads between 10-Year and 2-Year Government Bonds in Emerging East Asia

Source: *AsianBondsOnline* calculations based on Bloomberg LP data.

regarding US monetary policy, as some Federal Reserve officials became less dovish during the review period. In addition, the US elections raised market uncertainties as seen in the fluctuations in betting market probabilities. In contrast, Thailand's 10-year and 2-year spread fell despite a central bank rate cut as the Bank of Thailand indicated that its policy action was a "recalibration" and not the start of a new easing cycle. The central bank noted that financial conditions remain tight and expressed concern that high public debt levels would present a drag on economic growth.

Recent Developments in ASEAN+3 Sustainable Bond Markets

Sustainable Bonds Outstanding

Sustainable bonds outstanding in the ASEAN+3 bond market expanded at an accelerated pace in the third quarter (Q3) of 2024 to hit USD893.1 billion at the end of September, supported by increased issuance.[8]
In Q3 2024, ASEAN+3 sustainable bonds outstanding posted quarter-on-quarter (q-o-q) growth of 4.1%, compared with the previous quarter's 2.0%. The rate of expansion also outpaced that in the European Union 20 (EU-20) (1.9%) and the United States (1.2%) during the same period. The accelerated growth was largely supported by increased issuance in Q3 2024 amid improved financial conditions driven by monetary easing in both advanced economies and many regional markets. With the faster expansion, ASEAN+3's share of global sustainable bonds outstanding slightly rose to 18.9% at the end of Q3 2024 from 18.7% at the end of the previous quarter. Within the region, Hong Kong, China and the Association of Southeast Asian Nations (ASEAN) recorded the fastest q-o-q expansions of 11.6% and 9.2%, respectively. ASEAN+3 remained the second-largest regional sustainable bond market globally after the EU-20, which accounted for 36.4% of the global total (**Figure 14**). Nevertheless, ASEAN+3's sustainable bond market only comprised 2.3% of its general bond market at the end of September, lagging the EU-20's corresponding share of 7.9%.

ASEAN+3's sustainable bond market at the end of Q3 2024 largely comprised green instruments, private sector financing, and local currency (LCY) funding (Figure 15). This contrasts with ASEAN+3's general bond market, where the public sector and LCY financing

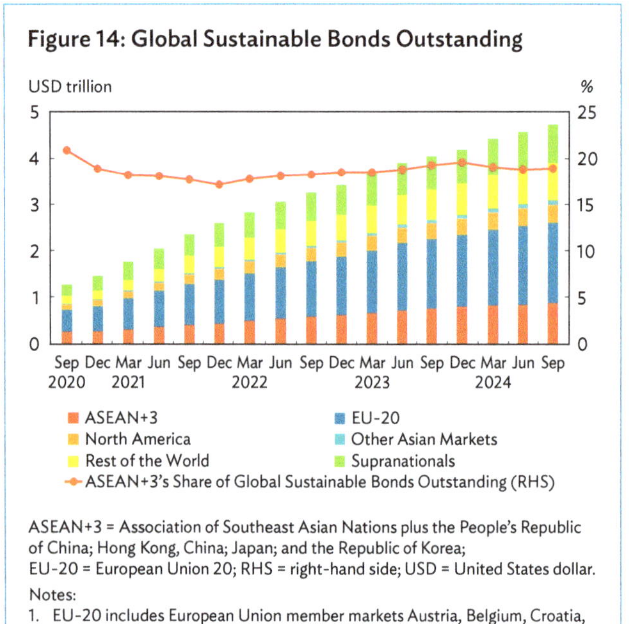

Figure 14: Global Sustainable Bonds Outstanding

ASEAN+3 = Association of Southeast Asian Nations plus the People's Republic of China; Hong Kong, China; Japan; and the Republic of Korea;
EU-20 = European Union 20; RHS = right-hand side; USD = United States dollar.
Notes:
1. EU-20 includes European Union member markets Austria, Belgium, Croatia, Cyprus, Estonia, Finland, France, Germany, Greece, Ireland, Italy, Latvia, Lithuania, Luxembourg, Malta, the Netherlands, Portugal, Slovakia, Slovenia, and Spain.
2. Data include both local currency and foreign currency issues.

Source: *AsianBondsOnline* calculations based on Bloomberg LP data.

Figure 15: Market Profile of Outstanding ASEAN+3 Sustainable Bonds at the End of September 2024

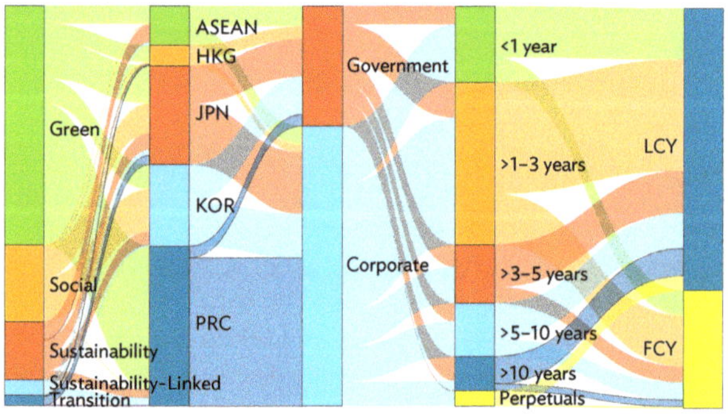

ASEAN = Association of Southeast Asian Nations; FCY = foreign currency; HKG = Hong Kong, China; JPN = Japan; KOR = Republic of Korea; LCY = local currency; PRC = People's Republic of China.
Notes:
1. ASEAN+3 is defined to include member states of ASEAN plus the People's Republic of China; Hong Kong, China; Japan; and the Republic of Korea.
2. ASEAN comprises the markets of Cambodia, Indonesia, the Lao People's Democratic Republic, Malaysia, the Philippines, Singapore, Thailand, and Viet Nam.
3. Sustainability-linked bonds include transition-linked bonds.

Source: *AsianBondsOnline* calculations based on Bloomberg LP data.

---

[8] ASEAN+3 is defined to include member states of the Association of Southeast Asian Nations (ASEAN) plus the People's Republic of China; Hong Kong, China; Japan; and the Republic of Korea.

dominate. At the end of Q3 2024, the private sector accounted for 70.0% of sustainable bonds outstanding in ASEAN+3, compared with its share of 25.4% in the ASEAN+3 general bond market. Such contrast, however, is not as apparent in the EU-20 market (**Table 3**). In the EU-20, the share of the private sector in the sustainable bond market stood at 50.8% at the end of Q3 2024, compared with its share of 39.6% in the EU-20 general bond market. Within ASEAN+3, Hong Kong, China and ASEAN markets have relatively higher shares of public sector participation, with the public sector accounting for 62.4% and 51.8% of total outstanding sustainable bonds, respectively, at the end of Q3 2024. Currency-wise, the share of LCY financing was lower in the ASEAN+3 sustainable bond market (70.5%) compared with its general bond market (95.1%), while in the EU-20 the LCY financing shares in both markets were similar at around 90%. Moreover, ASEAN markets have an active presence in the ASEAN+3 sustainable bond market, accounting for 9.8% of ASEAN+3 sustainable bonds outstanding at

the end of Q3 2024, which outpaced their corresponding share of 6.0% in the ASEAN+3 general bond market.

The ASEAN+3 sustainable bond market is dominated by short- to medium-term financing. Around 74% of ASEAN+3's sustainable bonds carry tenors of 5 years or less, which is much higher than the corresponding share of about 44% in the EU-20 sustainable bond market (**Figure 16**). As a result, the size-weighted average tenor of sustainable bonds in ASEAN+3 at the end of Q3 2024 (4.5 years) was just around half of that in the EU-20 (8.2 years). Maturities of 5 years or less were most prevalent among ASEAN+3's green and social bonds, with shares of 77.8% and 79.5%, respectively, at the end of September (**Figure 17**). In contrast, transition bonds and sustainability bonds had a greater share of longer tenors of more than 5 years (46.5% and 42.2%, respectively). Nearly two-thirds (64.3%) of sustainable bonds outstanding in ASEAN markets at the end of Q3 2024 had maturities of over 5 years, which was largely due to the strong participation of the public sector, particularly in Indonesia, the Philippines, Singapore, and Thailand. As a result, ASEAN sustainable bonds outstanding had a much longer

Table 3: Instrument, Issuer, and Currency Profiles in the ASEAN+3 and European Union 20 Sustainable Bond Markets at the End of the Third Quarter of 2024

	ASEAN+3	EU-20
Instrument profile (as a share of regional sustainable bonds outstanding)		
Green bonds	59.9%	65.0%
Social bonds	19.1%	17.6%
Sustainability bonds	14.5%	9.3%
SLBs (including transition-linked bonds)	3.9%	7.9%
Transition bonds	2.6%	0.3%
Issuer and currency profile		
Private sector (as a share of regional general bonds outstanding)	25.4%	39.6%
Private sector (as a share of regional sustainable bonds outstanding)	70.0%	50.8%
LCY financing (as a share of regional general bonds outstanding)	95.1%	89.4%
LCY financing (as a share of regional sustainable bonds outstanding)	70.5%	90.1%

ASEAN+3 = Association of Southeast Asian Nations plus the People's Republic of China; Hong Kong, China; Japan; and the Republic of Korea; EU-20 = European Union 20; LCY = local currency; SLB = sustainability-linked bond.

Source: *AsianBondsOnline* calculations based on Bloomberg LP data.

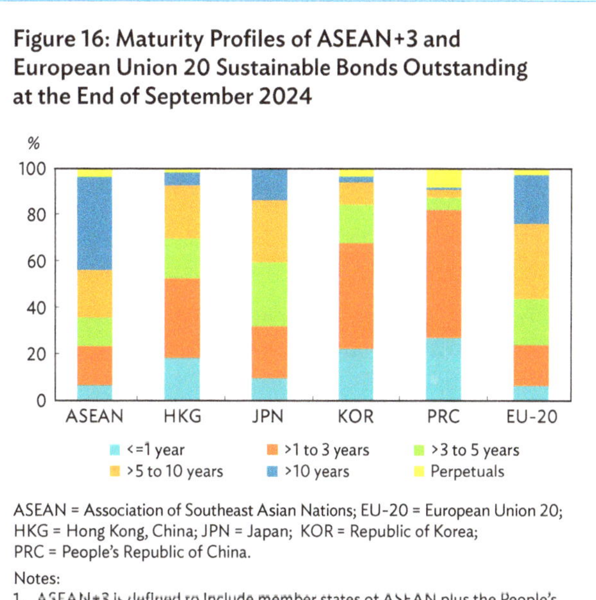

Figure 16: Maturity Profiles of ASEAN+3 and European Union 20 Sustainable Bonds Outstanding at the End of September 2024

ASEAN = Association of Southeast Asian Nations; EU-20 = European Union 20; HKG = Hong Kong, China; JPN = Japan; KOR = Republic of Korea; PRC = People's Republic of China.

Notes:
1. ASEAN+3 is defined to include member states of ASEAN plus the People's Republic of China; Hong Kong, China; Japan; and the Republic of Korea.
2. ASEAN comprises the markes of Cambodia, Indonesia, the Lao People's Democratic Republic, Malaysia, the Philippines, Singapore, Thailand, and Viet Nam.
3. The EU-20 includes European Union member markets Austria, Belgium, Croatia, Cyprus, Estonia, Finland, France, Germany, Greece, Ireland, Italy, Latvia, Lithuania, Luxembourg, Malta, the Netherlands, Portugal, Slovakia, Slovenia, and Spain.
4. Data include both local currency and foreign currency issues.

Source: *AsianBondsOnline* calculations based on Bloomberg LP data.

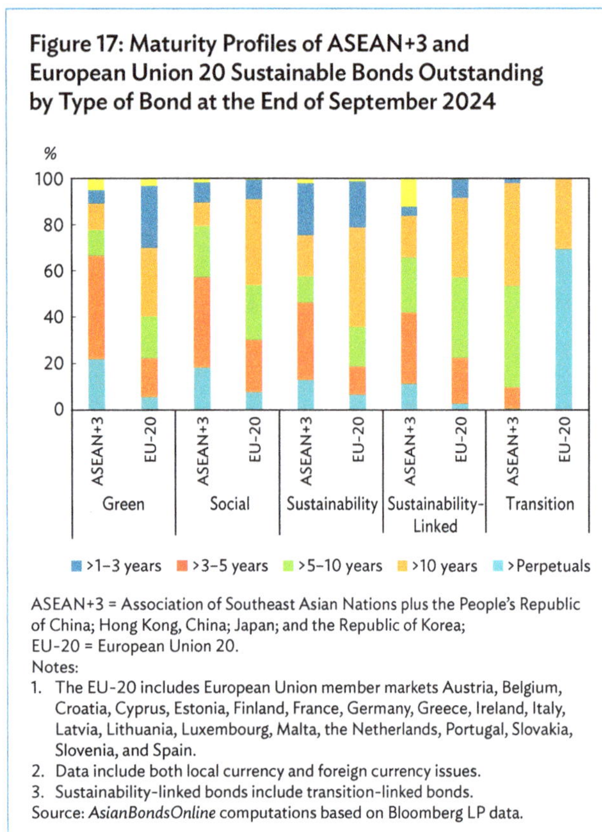

Figure 17: Maturity Profiles of ASEAN+3 and European Union 20 Sustainable Bonds Outstanding by Type of Bond at the End of September 2024

ASEAN+3 = Association of Southeast Asian Nations plus the People's Republic of China; Hong Kong, China; Japan; and the Republic of Korea; EU-20 = European Union 20.

Notes:
1. The EU-20 includes European Union member markets Austria, Belgium, Croatia, Cyprus, Estonia, Finland, France, Germany, Greece, Ireland, Italy, Latvia, Lithuania, Luxembourg, Malta, the Netherlands, Portugal, Slovakia, Slovenia, and Spain.
2. Data include both local currency and foreign currency issues.
3. Sustainability-linked bonds include transition-linked bonds.

Source: *AsianBondsOnline* computations based on Bloomberg LP data.

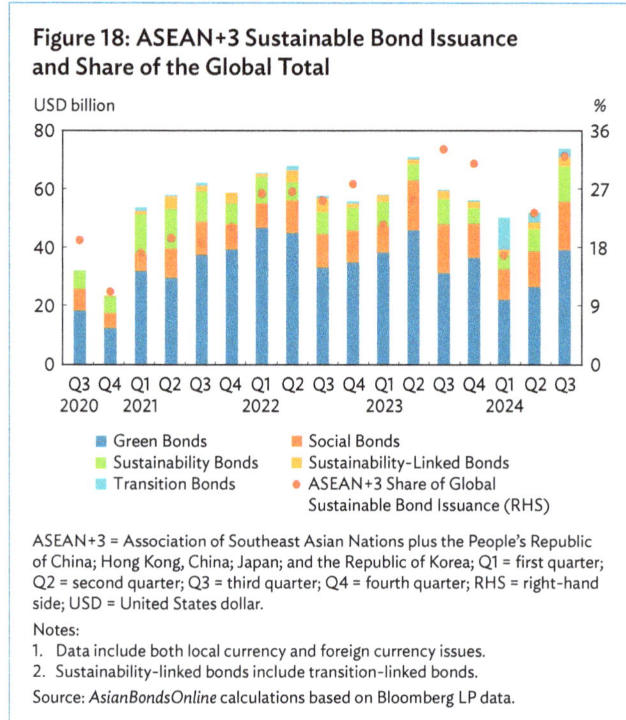

Figure 18: ASEAN+3 Sustainable Bond Issuance and Share of the Global Total

ASEAN+3 = Association of Southeast Asian Nations plus the People's Republic of China; Hong Kong, China; Japan; and the Republic of Korea; Q1 = first quarter; Q2 = second quarter; Q3 = third quarter; Q4 = fourth quarter; RHS = right-hand side; USD = United States dollar.

Notes:
1. Data include both local currency and foreign currency issues.
2. Sustainability-linked bonds include transition-linked bonds.

Source: *AsianBondsOnline* calculations based on Bloomberg LP data.

size-weighted average tenor of 11.5 years versus 4.5 years in ASEAN+3 markets. Singapore had the longest size-weighted average tenor for sustainable bonds across all ASEAN+3 markets (17.6 years), followed by the Philippines (12.9 years).

Sustainable Bond Issuance

ASEAN+3 sustainable bond issuance rose to an all-time high of USD73.7 billion in Q3 2024, with growth accelerating to 42.0% q-o-q from 3.5% q-o-q in the prior quarter. Supported by improved financial conditions amid monetary easing, growth in ASEAN+3 sustainable bond issuance in Q3 2024 outperformed that of the global sustainable bond market (3.3% q-o-q). As a result, ASEAN+3's share of global sustainable issuance rose to 31.9% in Q3 2024 from 23.2% in the previous quarter (**Figure 18**). All sustainable bond types in ASEAN+3 posted q-o-q gains in Q3 2024 except for transition bonds. The People's Republic of China was the region's largest issuer of green bonds in Q3 2024 with a 56.9% share, while the Republic of Korea was the largest issuer of social bonds with a 51.9% share. ASEAN markets were collectively the region's largest issuer of sustainability

bonds with a 39.1% share, while Japan was the biggest issuer of sustainability-linked bonds (39.4% share) and the only issuer of transition bonds during the quarter.

In Q3 2024, ASEAN+3's sustainable bond issuance mostly comprised LCY financing, private sector financing, and short- to medium-term financing (Figure 19).

- Around 67.7% of ASEAN+3 sustainable bond issuance in Q3 2024 was denominated in their respective local currency. This was well below the LCY issuance share of 94.6% in the ASEAN+3 general bond market during the quarter. Similar to outstanding bonds, LCY financing accounted for 87.8% of EU-20 sustainable bond issuance in Q3 2024. ASEAN markets had similar shares of LCY financing in sustainable bond issuance (68.1%) and general bond issuance (70.8%).
- Sustainable bond issuances with tenors of more than 5 years comprised 28.8% of ASEAN+3 total issuance in Q3 2024. The corresponding share was much higher in ASEAN markets, where tenors of 5 years or more represented 58.9% of total sustainable bond issuance during the quarter. The strong participation of the public sector partly contributed to the longer maturities of sustainable bond issuances in ASEAN economies. In Q3 2024, 64.3% of ASEAN public sector

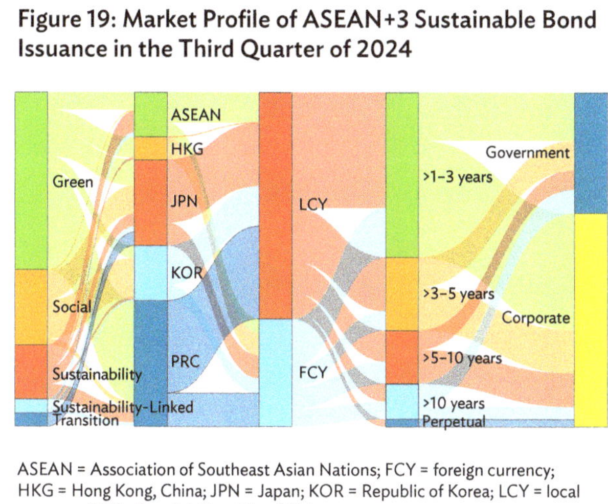

Figure 19: Market Profile of ASEAN+3 Sustainable Bond Issuance in the Third Quarter of 2024

ASEAN = Association of Southeast Asian Nations; FCY = foreign currency; HKG = Hong Kong, China; JPN = Japan; KOR = Republic of Korea; LCY = local currency; PRC = People's Republic of China.

Notes:
1. ASEAN+3 is defined to include member states of ASEAN plus the People's Republic of China; Hong Kong, China; Japan; and the Republic of Korea.
2. ASEAN comprises the markets of Indonesia, Malaysia, the Philippines, Singapore, Thailand, and Viet Nam.

Source: *AsianBondsOnline* calculations based on Bloomberg LP data.

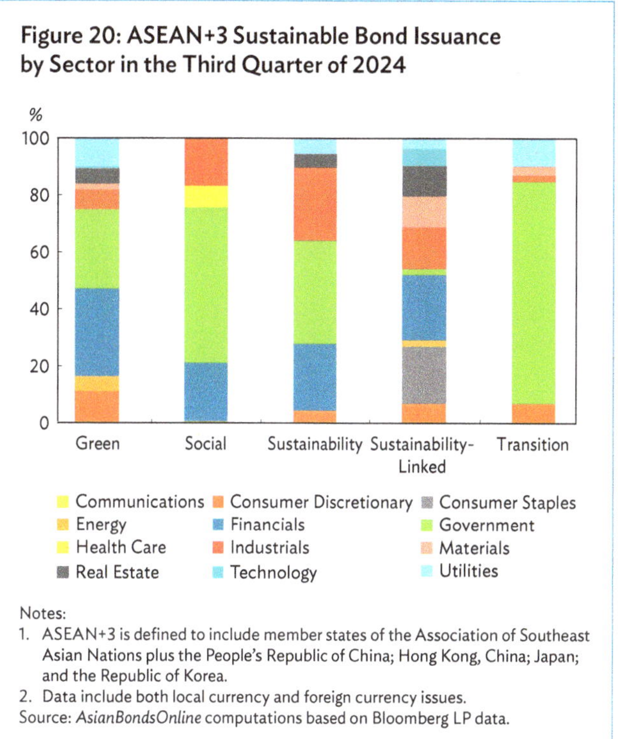

Figure 20: ASEAN+3 Sustainable Bond Issuance by Sector in the Third Quarter of 2024

Notes:
1. ASEAN+3 is defined to include member states of the Association of Southeast Asian Nations plus the People's Republic of China; Hong Kong, China; Japan; and the Republic of Korea.
2. Data include both local currency and foreign currency issues.

Source: *AsianBondsOnline* computations based on Bloomberg LP data.

issuance carried maturities of more than 10 years. The size-weighted average maturity of ASEAN sustainable bond issuance during the quarter stood at 14.1 years, which was almost double the size-weighted average of 7.6 years in the EU-20 and more than double the size-weighted average of 6.7 years in ASEAN+3.

- Only about 36% of ASEAN+3's sustainable bond issuance in Q3 2024 emanated from the public sector. Nevertheless, public sector issuance accounted for more than half (54%) of sustainable bonds issued during the quarter with maturities of over 10 years. Private sector sustainable bond issuance had a substantial presence among sustainability-linked bonds (SLBs) (98.0% of regional SLB issuance), green bonds (72.3% of regional green bond issuance), and sustainability bonds (63.7% of regional sustainability bond issuance) (**Figure 20**). Private sector sustainable bond issuance in Q3 2024 was led by firms from the financial (40.1%), industrial (19.1%), and consumer discretionary (11.1%) sectors. Meanwhile, the public sector led the issuance of social bonds (54.5%) and transition bonds (78.0%) during the quarter.

Sustainable bonds are useful tools to support transition-related activities in ASEAN+3. Following the approach of the International Capital Market Association, *AsianBondsOnline* tracks transition-related sustainable bonds, which comprise green bonds, sustainability bonds, and sustainability-linked bonds issued by the fossil fuels and hard-to-abate sectors (e.g., coal operations, power generation, airlines, chemicals, and metals and mining, among others), as well as transition bonds.[9] From the beginning of 2019 through the end of Q3 2024, cumulative issuance of transition-related sustainable bonds reached USD20.7 billion, accounting for 1.9% of the total issuance of ASEAN+3 sustainable bonds during the same period. Around 13.5% of total SLBs issued in the ASEAN+3 market originated from the fossil fuels sector and the hard-to-abate sector (22.2%). For cumulative green bond issuance in ASEAN+3 from January 2019 to September 2024, 14.8% came from the fossil fuels sector and 9.0% from the hard-to-abate sector (**Figure 21**). For sustainability bond issuance, 1.9% and 5.6% came from the fossil fuels and hard-to-abate sectors, respectively.

---

[9] International Capital Markets Association (ICMA). 2024. Transition Finance in the Debt Capital Market. *ICMA Staff Paper.*

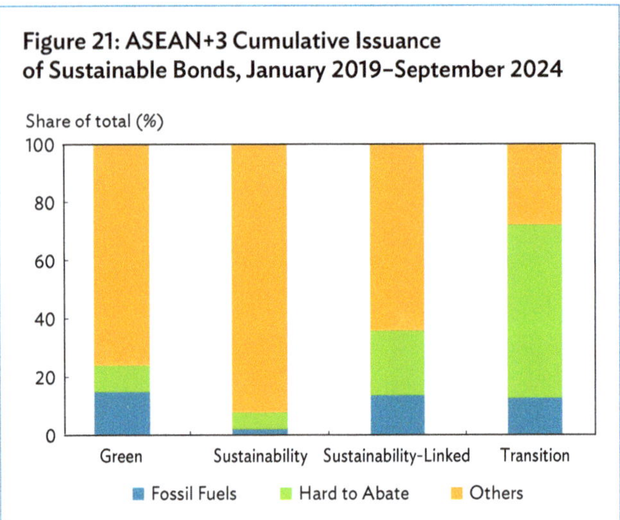

Figure 21: ASEAN+3 Cumulative Issuance of Sustainable Bonds, January 2019–September 2024

Notes:
1. ASEAN+3 is defined to include member states of the Association of Southeast Asian Nations plus the People's Republic of China; Hong Kong, China; Japan; and the Republic of Korea.
2. Data include both local currency and foreign currency issues.
3. Sustainability-linked bonds include transition-linked bonds.
Source: *AsianBondsOnline* computations based on Bloomberg LP data.

Policy and Regulatory Developments

People's Republic of China

People's Bank of China Reduces Reserve Requirement Ratio

The People's Bank of China in September reduced the reserve requirement ratio (RRR) by 50 basis points (bps). The move will bring the average RRR of the banking sector to 6.60%. The central bank stated that the move was meant to promote a monetary and financial environment conducive to growth of the domestic economy.

Hong Kong, China

Hong Kong Monetary Authority Lowers Countercyclical Capital Buffer Ratio to 0.5%

On 18 October, the Hong Kong Monetary Authority cut the countercyclical capital buffer (CCyB) ratio for banks in Hong Kong, China from 1.0% to 0.5%. The lower CCyB will release additional funds that banks can use to support the financing needs of the domestic economy, particularly small and medium-sized enterprises. The monetary authority noted that while the domestic economy recovers, sectors such as small and medium-sized businesses continue to face challenges amid uncertainties in both the domestic and global economic landscapes. The CCyB is an integral part of the Basel III regulatory capital framework designed to improve the resilience of the banking sector against system-wide risks.

Indonesia

2025 State Budget Bill Approved by Parliament

In September, the House of Representatives passed the 2025 State Budget Bill amounting to IDR3,621.1 trillion. With revenue collection projected at IDR3,005.1 trillion, the fiscal deficit is estimated to reach IDR616.2 trillion, equivalent to 2.5% of gross domestic product (GDP). This is lower compared with the 2024 state budget, which programmed a budget shortfall equivalent to 2.7% of GDP. Debt financing is projected to be IDR775.9 trillion, funded through bond issuances (IDR642.6 trillion) and loans (IDR133.3 trillion). Underlying macroeconomic assumptions for the 2025 state budget include: (i) GDP growth of 5.2%; (ii) an inflation rate of 2.5%; (iii) an exchange rate of IDR16,100 per USD1; and (iv) a 10-year government bond yield of 7.1%, among others.

Republic of Korea

FTSE Russell Announces the Republic of Korea's Inclusion in the World Government Bond Index in November 2025

On 8 October, the FTSE Russell announced its plan to include the Republic of Korea in the FTSE World Government Bond Index starting November 2025. This will be done in a phased approach to allow global market participants to prepare for the inclusion. Upon inclusion in the index, the Republic of Korea's inclusion ratio will also gradually increase over the following year. As of October 2024, the Republic of Korea's weight in the index upon inclusion is projected to be at 2.2%, which would be ranked the ninth largest among all included economies. The inclusion in the index is expected to stabilize bond yields and increase foreign exchange liquidity in the market to support the Korean won. However, FTSE Russell noted that the government's 50-year bonds will not be included due to their low liquidity and outstanding balance in the market.

Malaysia

Malaysia Announces 2025 Budget Spending Plan

On 18 October, the Government of Malaysia approved the proposed budget spending plan for 2025 amounting to MYR421.0 billion. This budget is approximately 3.3% greater than the 2024 budget and projects a fiscal deficit of around 3.8% of GDP, with an assumption of GDP growth of 4.5%–5.5% in 2025. State revenue, projected at MYR339.7 billion, will increase 5.5% from this year and will be supported by initiatives such as expanded sales and services tax, a carbon tax, and excise duties on sugary beverages.

Philippines

Bangko Sentral ng Pilipinas Cuts Reserve Requirement Ratio

Effective 25 October, the RRR for banks and nonbank financial institutions was reduced by 250 bps to 7.0%. The RRR for digital banks was also cut by 200 bps to 4.0%, while the RRRs for thrift banks and rural and cooperative banks were lowered by 100 bps to 1.0% and 0.0%, respectively. The adjustments are expected to lower intermediation costs and promote better pricing for financial services, aligning with the central bank's persistent efforts to reduce distortions in the financial system.

Bureau of Internal Revenue Issues Guidelines on *Sukuk* Taxation

In July, the Bureau of Internal Revenue issued guidelines on tax treatment for *sukuk* (Islamic bonds), which adhere to Sharia law and prohibit interest. Tax on *sukuk* will be based on gains or profits specified in the contracts, such as profit-sharing ratios, rental income, mark-up, price differentials, or the sale of underlying assets. *Sukuk* are also subject to a documentary stamp tax unless exempted. Banks will evaluate *sukuk* investments based on their contractual cash flow features and assess them for impairment based on expected credit losses. The tax treatment aims for neutrality between Islamic and conventional banking transactions.

Singapore

Singapore Continues Implementation of Green Plan 2030

On 25 September, Singapore's Ministry of Finance released the newest edition of the Singapore Green Bond Report. The latest report shows allocations for the Jurong Region Line and Cross Island Line in support of government efforts to position Singapore as a leader in sustainability. Launched in 2021, the Singapore Green Plan 2030 aims to advance Singapore's sustainable development goals. The recent allocations to finance the capital expenditures needed for the Jurong Region Line and Cross Island Line expand a major pillar in the project to advance mass public transportation.

Regional Central Banks Collaborate to Make Cross-Border Transactions More Efficient

On 28 October, the Monetary Authority of Singapore, along with the central banks of the Republic of Korea, Australia, and Malaysia, announced a partnership to improve efficiencies in cross-border payments. The initiative, entitled Project Mandala, seeks to simplify and streamline cross-border transactions by embedding market-specific regulatory and policy requirements into a unified compliance framework. This model aims to automate key compliance tasks such as anti-money laundering checks and foreign exchange regulations to reduce transaction delays and improve transparency.

Thailand

Thai Cabinet Approves Fiscal Year 2025 Public Debt Plan

On 1 October, the Thai cabinet approved a public debt management plan for fiscal year (FY) 2025. The government plans to borrow a total of THB3.6 trillion in FY2025, which started on 1 October 2024. About THB1.2 trillion was allotted for new borrowing, mainly to finance the budget deficit, while THB1.8 trillion was earmarked for debt restructuring and THB489.1 billion for debt repayment. The borrowing plan includes THB1.3 trillion of sovereign bonds, of which THB140.0 billion will be issued through bond switching, THB520.0 billion in Treasury bonds, THB120.0 billion in savings bonds, and the rest in promissory notes and term loans. Public debt is expected to reach 66.8% of GDP at the end of FY2025, which is below the legal limit of 70%.

Viet Nam

State Bank of Vietnam Amends Rules on Bills Issuance

On 30 August, the State Bank of Vietnam issued Circular No. 44 amending Circular No. 16 issued in 2019. The new circular includes general and specialized finance companies as part of the eligible entities that can buy and sell central bank bills. These entities will be added to the financial companies that belong to the regulated entities in Circular No. 16. This amendment will take effect on 23 October 2024.

State Bank of Vietnam Revises Rules on Banks' Sale and Purchase of Corporate Bonds

In June, the State Bank of Vietnam issued Circular No. 11 amending the regulation on mandatory principles and procedures relating to banks' sale and purchase of corporate bonds. Effective 12 August, banks must use noncash payment services when paying for traded corporate bonds. Furthermore, bond sellers must provide banks with information about related persons, in accordance with the Law on Credit Institutions, before the date on which the banks buy their bonds.

Digitalization in Green Bond Markets

Introduction to Digital Bond Markets

The bond market, a cornerstone of global financial markets, is undergoing a digital transformation. Blockchain technology and distributed-ledger technology (DLT) provide tamper-proof and secure ledgers, enabling more efficient and transparent transactions in the issuance and trading of bonds. This transition from traditional to digital bond markets is particularly significant for green bonds, which fund environmentally sustainable projects.

Digitalization offers several key benefits for green bond markets. Blockchain's immutable ledger minimizes the risk of fraud and unauthorized data alterations, significantly enhancing security. By automating manual processes and eliminating intermediaries, blockchain reduces underwriting fees, administrative overhead, and other transaction costs. Blockchain facilitates fractional ownership of bonds, allowing smaller investors to participate in the market, thereby increasing liquidity and inclusivity.

While the potential benefits of digital bonds are substantial, there are challenges, including regulatory uncertainty, interoperability among blockchain platforms, and technical complexities in integrating blockchain with existing systems. Addressing these challenges is crucial for the widespread adoption of digital bonds.

Theoretical Background: Resource-Based and Dynamic Capability Theories

This special section is based on two key theoretical frameworks to explain the role of blockchain in green bond markets: resource-based theory (RBT) and dynamic capability theory (DCT).

RBT posits that firms gain a competitive advantage by leveraging their unique resources. Blockchain technology—with its secure, transparent, and decentralized structure—provides firms with a valuable resource in the green bond market. The transparency and trust facilitated by blockchain can differentiate firms and attract investors who prioritize security and environmental impact.

DCT complements RBT by focusing on a firm's ability to adapt to rapidly changing environments. In green bond markets, where regulations and investor expectations are continuously evolving, blockchain allows firms to adjust processes dynamically. By integrating blockchain, firms can respond more effectively to regulatory shifts, meet the increasing demand for transparency, and maintain their competitive edge.

These two theories suggest that firms that adopt blockchain technology in the issuance of green bonds not only improve their operational efficiency but also enhance their ability to navigate evolving market demands and regulations.

Literature Review: Benefits of Blockchain in Green Bond Markets

The paper this special section is based on synthesizes numerous empirical studies that highlight the benefits of integrating blockchain and DLT into green bond markets. These benefits include cost reduction, enhanced transparency and security, and increased market liquidity.

Cost Reduction

Blockchain significantly reduces the costs associated with bond issuance and trading. Studies by Leung, Wang, and Wong (2023) and Javaid (2022) show that tokenization of bonds through blockchain lowers underwriting fees, borrowing costs, and administrative overhead by automating many processes and eliminating intermediaries.

This special section was written by Suk Hyun (head professor) at the Graduate School of Environmental Finance of Yonsei University in the Republic of Korea.

Leung, Wang, and Wong (2023) find that blockchain reduces the costs of bond issuance by automating complex processes that traditionally require significant manual intervention. Javaid (2022) highlights how digital securities, facilitated by blockchain, offer faster and more cost-effective issuance, making green bonds more attractive to both issuers and investors.

The reduction in transaction costs and the acceleration of bond issuance processes make digital bonds a more efficient and cost-effective option for financing green projects.

Transparency and Security

One of the most significant advantages of blockchain is its ability to provide transparency and security in green bond transactions. According to Christodoulou, Lafond, and Wilson (2023), transparency is crucial in green bond markets to ensure that funds are allocated to genuine environmental projects. Blockchain's decentralized ledger system allows real-time tracking of bond proceeds, reducing the risk of "greenwashing" (i.e., the misuse of funds meant for environmental purposes).

Moreover, blockchain enhances security by making unauthorized data alterations virtually impossible. This reduces the risk of fraud, further boosting investor confidence in the integrity of green bond markets. Investors can trust that their funds are being used appropriately, knowing that blockchain ensures full transparency and accountability.

Liquidity and Market Accessibility

Blockchain's ability to enhance liquidity and market accessibility is another significant advantage. By enabling fractional ownership of bonds, blockchain allows smaller investors to enter markets that were previously dominated by large institutional players. Trivedi (2021) explains that this fractionalization increases liquidity by lowering the entry barriers for investors and enabling bonds to be traded more frequently.

Furthermore, blockchain's real-time settlement capabilities reduce delays and counterparty risks, enhancing the overall efficiency of bond markets. Parker and Scott (2021) also highlight how 24/7 trading capabilities provided by blockchain platforms enhance liquidity, making the bond market more attractive to a broader range of investors.

Case Studies: Practical Applications of Blockchain in Green Bond Markets

The paper this special section is based on presents two case studies from Japan and Hong Kong, China to illustrate the practical applications of blockchain technology in the issuance of green bonds.

Japan Exchange Group's Digitally Tracked Green Bonds

Japan Exchange Group (JPX) has introduced a groundbreaking initiative by issuing digitally tracked green bonds. These bonds, designed to finance environmentally sustainable projects, use blockchain technology to track and report the environmental impact of the financed projects in real-time. Key features of this initiative are discussed below.

Blockchain allows investors to monitor the environmental outcomes of their investments in real-time, ensuring transparency in the use of proceeds. In collaboration with Hitachi, JPX developed the Green Tracking Hub, which provides investors with data on the environmental performance of the projects funded by the bonds.

JPX's initiative demonstrates how blockchain can improve the accountability and transparency of green financing, increasing investor confidence in the integrity of green bond projects.

Hong Kong, China's Digital Green Bonds

In 2023, the Government of the Hong Kong Special Administrative Region of the People's Republic of China issued the world's first tokenized green bond as part of its Government Green Bond Programme. This issuance, valued at HKD800 million, was conducted using blockchain technology and smart contracts, resulting in several key benefits.

These automated smart contracts facilitated bond issuance, settlement, and redemption, significantly reducing transaction times. The settlement period for these bonds was reduced to T+1 days from the T+2 or

T+3 days typical of traditional bond markets. The bonds were tokenized and issued using the Hong Kong Monetary Authority's digital currency, referred to as e-HKD, demonstrating Hong Kong, China's commitment to integrating digital solutions into its financial infrastructure.

The successful issuance of these tokenized green bonds also highlights Hong Kong, China's leadership in both green finance and fintech innovation, setting a new standard for global bond markets.

Empirical Analysis: Liquidity and Efficiency Gains in Digital Bond Markets

This chapter provides empirical evidence demonstrating the growing adoption of digital bonds globally, particularly between 2020 and 2024. Over this period, more than USD3 billion in digital bonds was issued, reflecting the increasing role of blockchain technology in global financial markets. The table below summarizes the total issuance amounts of digital bonds over the 5-year review period.

Table 4 shows a clear upward trend in the issuance of digital bonds during the review period, with the exception of a minor dip in 2022. This growth indicates a significant shift toward the adoption of digital solutions in bond markets, driven by the advantages of blockchain technology in terms of efficiency, transparency, and security.

Key Findings: Liquidity and Efficiency Gains in Digital Bonds

Figure 22 provides empirical results that compare the liquidity and efficiency of digital bonds to conventional bonds. The metrics analyzed include bid–ask spread, yield spread, and yield to maturity (YTM).

The bid–ask spread is defined as the difference between the bid price and the ask price. The bid–ask spread for digital bonds is 0.16 percentage points lower than that of conventional bonds, indicating significantly higher liquidity for digital bonds. The t-statistic for this estimate is –6.04, indicating statistical significance at the 1% level.

The yield spread is defined as the difference between the yield on a bond and the risk-free rate. The yield spread for digital bonds is 0.62 percentage points lower than that for conventional bonds. This pronounced decline suggests that digital bonds are perceived as less risky, or more desirable, resulting in reduced yields. The t-statistic for this estimate is –9.75, which is also significant at the 1% level.

The YTM is defined as the expected return on an investment, given current market conditions and the investment's specific characteristics. The YTM for digital bonds is 0.42 percentage points lower than that for conventional bonds. This further supports the notion that digital bonds offer efficiency gains. The t-statistic for this estimate is –2.69, which is significant at the 5% level.

Table 4: Global Digital Bond Issuances by Year

Year	Issuance Amount (USD billion)
2020	0.50
2021	1.11
2022	0.82
2023	1.01
2024	1.20
Total	**4.64**

USD = United States dollar.
Source: Bloomberg.

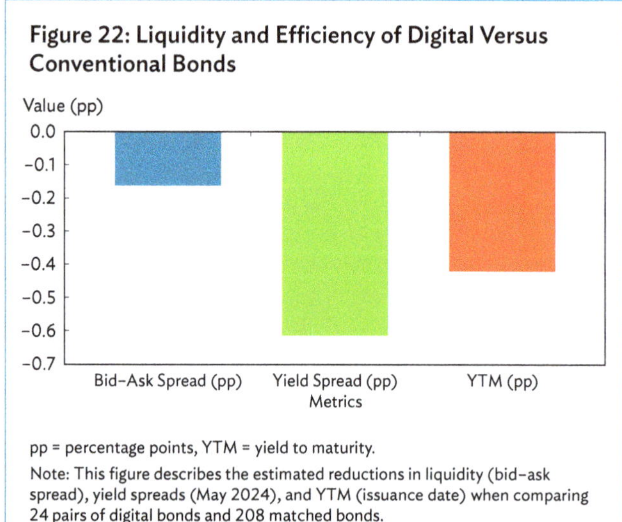

Figure 22: Liquidity and Efficiency of Digital Versus Conventional Bonds

pp = percentage points, YTM = yield to maturity.
Note: This figure describes the estimated reductions in liquidity (bid–ask spread), yield spreads (May 2024), and YTM (issuance date) when comparing 24 pairs of digital bonds and 208 matched bonds.
Source: Author's calculations.

Digital bonds exhibit superior liquidity and efficiency compared to conventional bonds. The lower bid–ask spreads, yield spreads, and YTM collectively indicate that digital bonds provide significant advantages in terms of trading efficiency and cost-effectiveness.

Summary and Implications

This study reveals meaningful insights into the potential of blockchain technology to optimize green bond market operations. Blockchain and DLT offer significant benefits in terms of efficiency, transparency, security, and accessibility in bond markets. These technologies can play a crucial role in preventing greenwashing by ensuring the accurate and transparent tracking of green bond proceeds. However, several challenges must be addressed to fully realize their potential. These include technical complexities, regulatory uncertainties, interoperability issues, and privacy concerns. Continued research and collaboration among market participants, regulators, and technology providers in the ASEAN+3 region is essential to addressing these challenges and promoting the broader adoption of blockchain technology in bond markets.[10]

Policymakers and industry leaders have a critical role to play in shaping the future of green finance by developing supportive policies and infrastructure that foster the adoption of blockchain technology. By doing so, they can help scale up sustainable finance efforts and contribute to the global fight against climate change through more efficient and transparent financial instruments.

References

K. Christodoulou, F. Lafond, and C. Wilson. 2023. Blockchain Technology and Green Bonds: Enhancing Transparency and Accountability. *Renewable Energy* 197. pp. 1247–60.

M. Javaid. 2022. The Role of Blockchain in Transforming Digital Securities: Enhancing Market Efficiency. *Journal of Digital Finance* 10 (4). pp. 350–69.

A. Leung, T. Wang, and K. Wong. 2023. Tokenization of Bonds and Cost Reduction: Evidence from Digital Securities. *Financial Review* 58 (1). pp. 25–39.

C. Parker, and M. Scott. 2021. Enhancing Market Accessibility through Blockchain: The Case of Fractional Ownership in Green Bonds. *Journal of Economic Perspectives* 35 (3). pp. 215–32.

A. Trivedi. 2021. Blockchain Technology in Green Bond Markets: Enhancing Transparency and Reducing Costs. *Journal of Sustainable Finance* 10 (2). pp. 183–99.

---

[10] ASEAN+3 is defined to include the member states of the Association of Southeast Asian Nations (ASEAN) plus the People's Republic of China; Hong Kong, China; Japan; and the Republic of Korea.

Market Summaries

People's Republic of China

Yield Movements

The People's Republic of China's (PRC) local currency (LCY) government bond yield curve rose for most tenors between 2 September and 31 October on expectations of an increased bond supply as the government enacted stimulus measures. Bond yields in the PRC rose an average of 1.4 basis points (bps) during the review period for most tenors at the longer end (4 years or longer) (**Figure 1**). All maturities of 3 years or less and the 7-year bond saw an average decline of 3.5 bps in the same period. The decline in the yield curve at the shorter end of the curve was supported by the People's Bank of China's (PBOC) aggressive monetary policy easing as it reduced a number of key rates.[11] Other easing measures were announced such as cuts in the reserve requirement ratio by 50 bps on 27 September. Support measures for the property sector and the stock market were announced on 23 September. The Government of the PRC, on 12 October and 18 October, also announced targeted measures such as additional quotas for local governments, more special sovereign bond issuances, and a recapitalization plan for state-owned banks. As a result, yields rose at the longer end of the curve over the prospects of an increased bond supply and a widening fiscal deficit as the government seeks to support the domestic economy. Gross domestic product growth fell to 4.6% year-on-year (y-o-y) in the third quarter (Q3) of 2024 from 4.7% y-o-y in the second quarter (Q2), both of which were down from the first quarter's 5.3% y-o-y growth rate. Consumer price inflation remained low, slightly easing from 0.6% y-o-y in August to 0.4% y-o-y in September and 0.3% y-o-y in October in another indication of weak domestic demand.

Local Currency Bond Market Size and Issuance

LCY bonds outstanding in the PRC grew at an accelerated pace in Q3 2024 on increased government bond issuance to reach CNY149.7 trillion at the end of September. Total LCY bonds outstanding grew 3.1% quarter-on-quarter (q-o-q) in Q3 2024, up from Q2 2024's 2.2% q-o-q growth (**Figure 2**). This was driven by accelerated growth in government bonds to 4.2% q-o-q in Q3 2024 from 2.8% q-o-q in Q2 2024.

Figure 1: The People's Republic of China's Benchmark Yield Curve—Local Currency Government Bonds

Source: Based on data from Bloomberg LP.

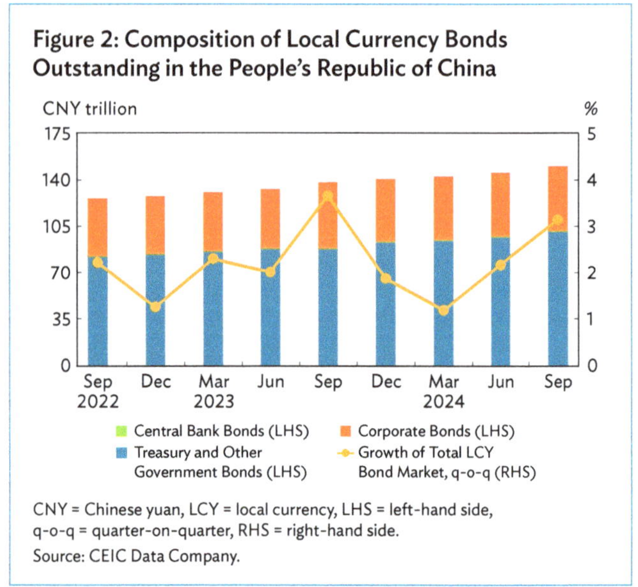

Figure 2: Composition of Local Currency Bonds Outstanding in the People's Republic of China

CNY = Chinese yuan, LCY = local currency, LHS = left-hand side, q-o-q = quarter-on-quarter, RHS = right-hand side.
Source: CEIC Data Company.

This market summary was written by Russ Jason Lo, consultant, Economic Research and Development Impact Department, ADB, Manila.

[11] On 25 September, the PBOC reduced the 1-year medium-term lending facility rate by 30 bps to 2.00%. On 27 September, it reduced the 7-day repurchase rate by 20 bps to 1.50%. On 21 October, the 1-year and 5-year loan prime rates were lowered by 25 bps each to 3.10% and 3.60%, respectively.

Corporate bonds also saw their growth rate inch up to 1.1% q-o-q, from 0.9% q-o-q in the previous quarter, over reduced funding costs.

Total bond sales in the PRC for Q3 2024 tallied CNY13.9 trillion, with q-o-q growth slightly down to 18.5% from the prior quarter's 21.3% due to a high base effect (Figure 3). While the PRC's government bonds showed healthy growth of 24.5% q-o-q in Q3 2024, this was down from the previous quarter's 32.2% q-o-q expansion. Both the central government and local governments continued to issue bonds to help support the domestic economy during the quarter. Corporate bond issuance growth was relatively stable at 10.4% q-o-q in Q3 2024 compared with 9.2% q-o-q in Q2 2024.

Investor Profile

The PRC's investor profile remained roughly the same at the end of September from a year earlier in terms of the respective shares of investor groups (Figure 4). Commercial banks remained the largest investor in the PRC's Treasury bond market with a share of 68.1% at the end of September, roughly the same as their 69.6% share a year earlier. Due to a high concentration of holdings among banking institutions, the PRC had emerging East Asia's second-highest score in the Herfindahl–Hirschman Index in Q3 2024, indicating relatively less diversity in its investor profile.[12]

Sustainable Bond Market

The private sector is a significant issuer of sustainable bonds in the PRC, mostly in the form of shorter-term instruments. The PRC has the largest sustainable bond market in the region, with a size of USD356.3 billion at the end of September, representing 39.9% of the emerging East Asian total. In contrast with the general bond market, the public sector is not an active participant in the sustainable bond market of the PRC, accounting for only 7.0% of bonds outstanding (**Figure 5**). Due to limited public sector participation, sustainable bonds in the PRC tend to be shorter-term instruments, with 87.8% of the PRC's sustainable bonds having tenors of 5 years or less. LCY financing also dominates the PRC's sustainable bond market, with a 78.1% share of the total.

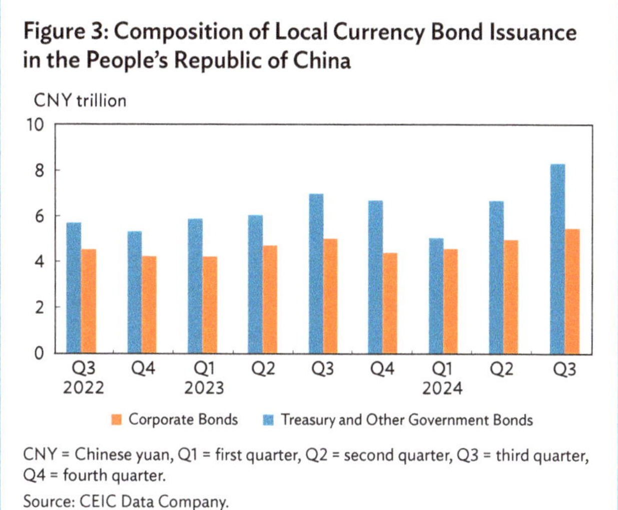

Figure 3: Composition of Local Currency Bond Issuance in the People's Republic of China

CNY = Chinese yuan, Q1 = first quarter, Q2 = second quarter, Q3 = third quarter, Q4 = fourth quarter.
Source: CEIC Data Company.

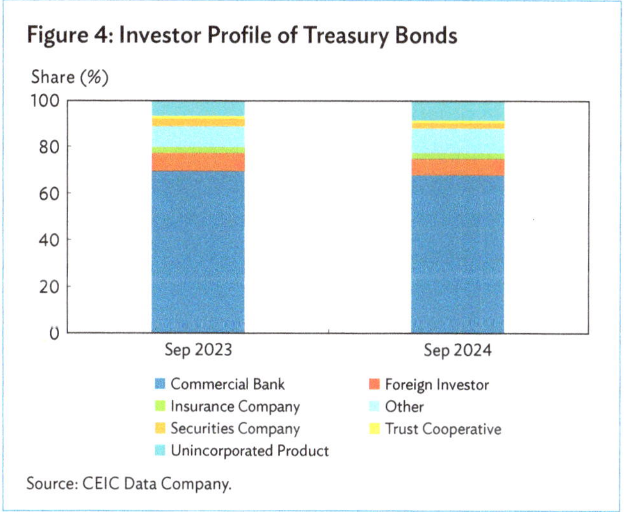

Figure 4: Investor Profile of Treasury Bonds

Source: CEIC Data Company.

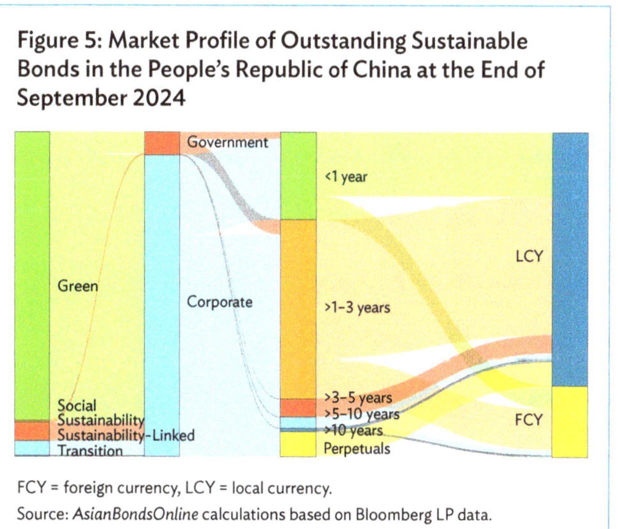

Figure 5: Market Profile of Outstanding Sustainable Bonds in the People's Republic of China at the End of September 2024

FCY = foreign currency, LCY = local currency.
Source: *AsianBondsOnline* calculations based on Bloomberg LP data.

---

[12] Emerging East Asia is defined to include member states of the Association of Southeast Asian Nations (ASEAN) plus the People's Republic of China; Hong Kong, China; and the Republic of Korea. The Herfindahl–Hirschman Index is a commonly accepted measure of market concentration. In this case, the index was used to measure the investor profile diversification of the LCY bond market and is calculated by summing the squared share of each investor group in the bond market.

Hong Kong, China

Yield Movements

Between 2 September and 31 October, local currency (LCY) government bond yields in Hong Kong, China were mostly up amid domestic and external policy developments. Bond yields rose at both the short and long ends of the curve but fell for a few short-term maturities (**Figure 1**). On average, LCY government bond yields rose by 10 basis points across all maturities. Yields rose at the short end of the curve (1-month, 3-month, and 6-month bonds) as the announcement of fiscal stimulus measures and monetary easing in the People's Republic of China fueled demand for equities and lowered demand for short-term bonds. Meanwhile, yields for 9-month, 1-year, and 3-year bonds fell, driven by monetary policy easing in the United States (US) and the subsequent reduction of the base rate by the Hong Kong Monetary Authority. Yields of bonds with maturities of 10 years and longer edged up, following trends in US Treasury yields. The prospect of an increased supply of longer-term bonds, as the Government of the Hong Kong Special Administrative Region (HKSAR) of the People's Republic of China develops its infrastructure and sustainable bond programs, may have also contributed to the uptick in longer-term bond yields.

Local Currency Bond Market Size and Issuance

Hong Kong, China's LCY bond market contracted 1.7% quarter-on-quarter (q-o-q) in the third quarter (Q3) of 2024 due to maturities in HKSAR government bonds and a decline in corporate bonds. Total LCY bonds outstanding inched down to HKD2,983.1 billion at the end of September from HKD3,033.6 billion at the end of June (**Figure 2**). Outstanding HKSAR bonds declined 14.2% q-o-q as HKD37.9 billion worth of bonds matured. Corporate bonds outstanding fell 1.8% q-o-q as issuance continued to decline amid uncertainties. Meanwhile, the stock of Exchange Fund Bills and Notes (EFBNs) posted a modest expansion of 1.0% q-o-q. Corporate bonds (HKD1,466.4 billion) accounted for almost half of the LCY bond market at the end of September. EFBNs (HKD1,294.7 billion) and HKSAR bonds (HKD222.1 billion) represented the remaining 43.4% and 7.4% shares, respectively.

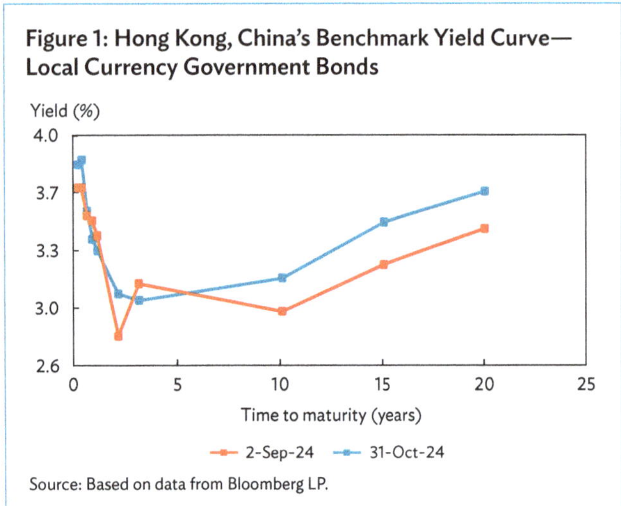

Figure 1: Hong Kong, China's Benchmark Yield Curve—Local Currency Government Bonds

Source: Based on data from Bloomberg LP.

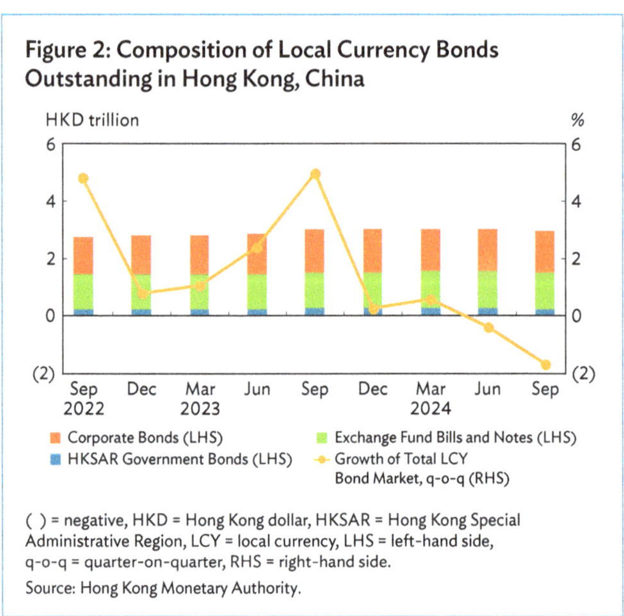

Figure 2: Composition of Local Currency Bonds Outstanding in Hong Kong, China

( ) = negative, HKD = Hong Kong dollar, HKSAR = Hong Kong Special Administrative Region, LCY = local currency, LHS = left-hand side, q-o-q = quarter-on-quarter, RHS = right-hand side.
Source: Hong Kong Monetary Authority.

LCY bond sales inched down 0.1% q-o-q in Q3 2024 amid a fall in issuance of corporate bonds. LCY bond issuance tallied HKD1,273.6 billion in Q3 2024 (**Figure 3**). Corporate bond sales continued to contract, falling 7.4% q-o-q in Q3 2024 as geopolitical tensions and interest rate uncertainties dampened investor confidence. Hong Kong Mortgage Corporation remained the top nonbank corporate issuer in Q3 2024, with total bond sales worth HKD16.5 billion, representing 40.8% of total nonbank issuance during the quarter. Meanwhile, issuance of EFBNs ticked up 1.7% q-o-q to HKD1,034.5 billion in Q3 2024. HKSAR government bond sales were steady at HK1.5 billion in both the second and third quarters of 2024, amid the transition from the existing Government Bond Programme to the new Government Sustainable Bond Programme and Infrastructure Bond Programme.

Sustainable Bond Market

Green bond instruments issued by the public sector continued to comprise a majority of Hong Kong, China's sustainable bond market. The sustainable bond market reached a size of USD46.6 billion at the end of Q3 2024, up 11.6% q-o-q on robust issuance. Green bonds were the predominant type of sustainable instrument, comprising an 83.4% share of the sustainable bond market, followed by social bonds (9.0%) and transition bonds (4.2%) (**Figure 4**). Government-issued sustainable bonds were all in the form of green bonds, totaling USD29.1 billion. Outstanding sustainable bonds were largely short- to medium-term instruments: the size-weighted average tenor of outstanding instruments was 4.6 years and about 70.0% of outstanding sustainable bonds had remaining maturities of up to 5 years. Among emerging East Asian markets, Hong Kong, China's sustainable bond market had one of the highest shares of foreign-currency-denominated bonds.[13] About 77.7% of outstanding sustainable bonds in Hong Kong, China were denominated in foreign currencies, as the government issues multicurrency green bonds to promote sustainable finance and strengthen its position as a sustainable finance hub. In Q3 2024, the Government of the Hong Kong Special Administrative Region of the People's Republic of China issued the equivalent of USD3.2 billion of green bonds denominated in US dollars, Chinese yuan, and euros.

Figure 3: Composition of Local Currency Bond Issuance in Hong Kong, China

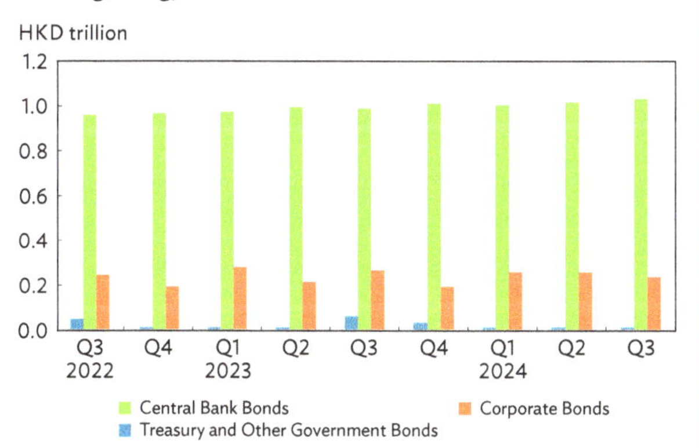

HKD = Hong Kong dollar, Q1 = first quarter, Q2 = second quarter, Q3 = third quarter, Q4 = fourth quarter.

Source: Hong Kong Monetary Authority.

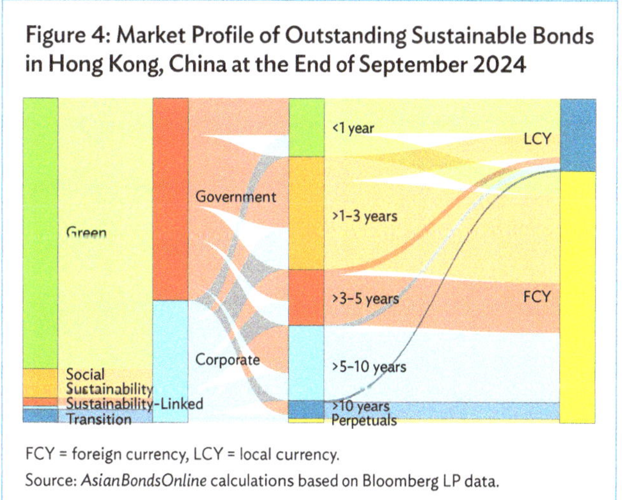

Figure 4: Market Profile of Outstanding Sustainable Bonds in Hong Kong, China at the End of September 2024

FCY = foreign currency, LCY = local currency.

Source: *AsianBondsOnline* calculations based on Bloomberg LP data.

---

[13] Emerging East Asia is defined to include member states of the Association of Southeast Asian Nations (ASEAN) plus the People's Republic of China; Hong Kong, China; and the Republic of Korea.

Indonesia

Yield Movements

Local currency (LCY) government bond yields in Indonesia climbed for most maturities from 2 September to 31 October, largely tracking the yield movements of United States Treasuries. Sovereign bond yields rose an average of 15 basis points (bps) for maturities of over 2 years, while yields fell by an average of 8 bps for tenors of 2 years or less (**Figure 1**). The uptick in yields was largely driven by uncertainties over the pace of the United States Federal Reserve's monetary policy easing as well as some domestic concerns over the policy direction of the new government. While Bank Indonesia reduced rates by 25 bps in its meeting in September, volatility in the domestic currency amid ongoing uncertainties led the central bank to hold rates steady at its meeting on 15–16 October. Nonetheless, continued moderation in inflation supported declining yields at the shorter end of the curve. Consumer price inflation eased to 1.8% year-on-year and 1.7% year-on-year in September and October, respectively, and is now approaching the lower end of the central bank's full-year 2024 target range of 1.5%–3.5%.

Local Currency Bond Market Size and Issuance

The LCY bond market in Indonesia reached a size of IDR7,545.6 trillion at the end of September, with growth moderating to 4.8% quarter-on-quarter (q-o-q) in the third quarter (Q3) of 2024 from 6.1% q-o-q in the second quarter (Q2). Much of the growth was contributed by government bonds, which expanded 2.3% q-o-q in Q3 2024, versus 1.6% q-o-q in the prior quarter, as improved domestic financial conditions supported new issuance (**Figure 2**). While central bank bonds posted the fastest rate of expansion among all bond types at 28.3% q-o-q, growth moderated from 69.1% q-o-q in Q2 2024. On the other hand, the corporate bond stock contracted (–1.7% q-o-q) over a high volume of maturities and reduced issuance in Q3 2024.

Total LCY bond issuance tallied IDR775.1 trillion in Q3 2024, with growth largely supported by government bonds (Figure 3). Overall issuance growth decelerated to 1.9% q-o-q in Q3 2024 from 12.3% q-o-q in Q2 2024. Growth was largely driven by government bond issuance

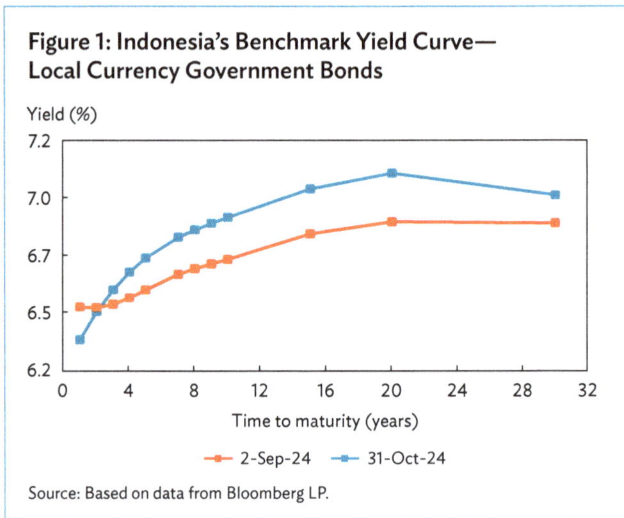

Figure 1: Indonesia's Benchmark Yield Curve—Local Currency Government Bonds

Source: Based on data from Bloomberg LP.

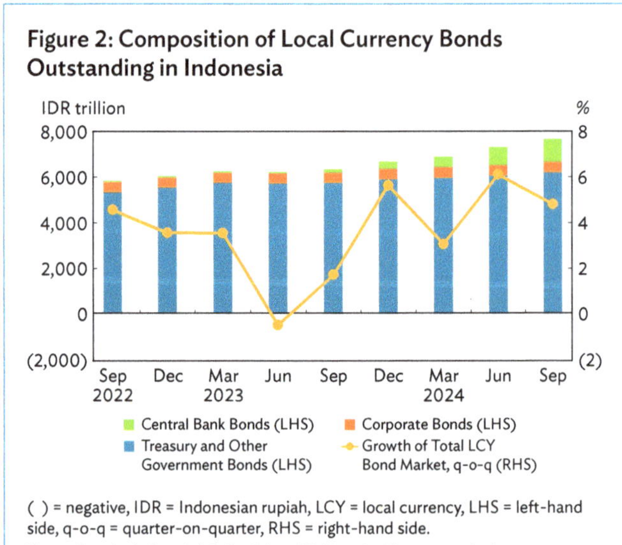

Figure 2: Composition of Local Currency Bonds Outstanding in Indonesia

( ) = negative, IDR = Indonesian rupiah, LCY = local currency, LHS = left-hand side, q-o-q = quarter-on-quarter, RHS = right-hand side.
Notes: Data include *sukuk* (Islamic bonds). Data for Treasury and other government bonds comprise tradable and nontradable central government bonds.
Sources: Bank Indonesia; Directorate General of Budget Financing and Risk Management, Ministry of Finance; and Indonesia Stock Exchange.

as improved financial conditions allowed the government to raise more funds and take advantage of declining borrowing costs. Growth in government bond issuance picked up to 26.3% q-o-q in Q3 2024 after contracting 23.4% q-o-q in the prior quarter. Central bank issuance contracted 6.2% q-o-q as financial conditions largely stabilized during Q3 2024, leading the central bank to reduce its issuance. Corporate bond issuance also contracted 9.8% q-o-q in Q3 2024.

This market summary was written by Roselyn Regalado, consultant, Economic Research and Development Impact Department, ADB, Manila.

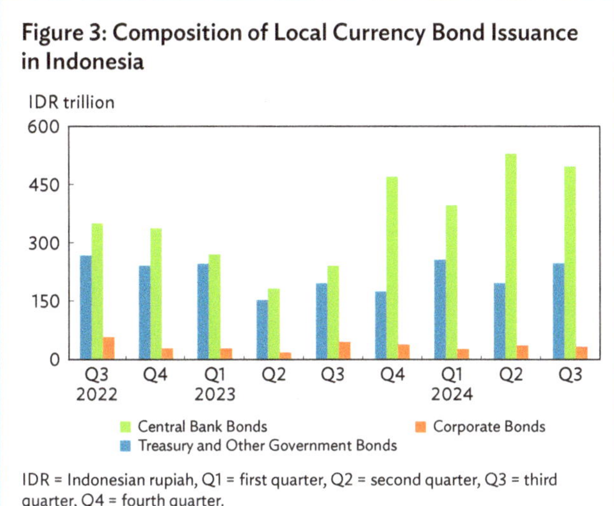

Figure 3: Composition of Local Currency Bond Issuance in Indonesia

IDR = Indonesian rupiah, Q1 = first quarter, Q2 = second quarter, Q3 = third quarter, Q4 = fourth quarter.

Notes: Data include *sukuk* (Islamic bonds). Data for Treasury and other government bonds comprise tradable and nontradable central government bonds.

Sources: Bank Indonesia; Directorate General of Budget Financing and Risk Management, Ministry of Finance; and Indonesia Stock Exchange.

Investor Profile

As with other emerging East Asian peers, LCY tradable sovereign bonds in Indonesia were largely held by domestic investors (85.3%).[14] However, unlike its regional peers, the largest bondholder in Indonesia was the central bank with a holdings share of 25.0% at the end of September. Bank Indonesia has gradually increased its holdings of government bonds to optimize its money market operations, as well as to support bond market stability. The next largest bondholders were banking institutions, which recorded a substantial decline in their holdings share to 19.5% at the end of September from

29.7% a year earlier. Meanwhile, foreign investors' holdings share ticked down to 14.7% at the end of September from 15.0% a year earlier despite a 5.8% increase in foreign holdings in nominal terms during the same period. By type of bond, the share of foreign ownership of conventional bonds at the end of September was much higher at 17.9% compared with 1.4% for *sukuk* (Islamic bonds) (**Figure 4**).

Sustainable Bond Market

The sustainable bond market in Indonesia largely comprises green bond instruments, public sector financing, and long-term tenors. Sustainable bonds outstanding in Indonesia reached USD13.7 billion at the end of September on accelerated growth of 10.2% q-o-q in Q3 2024, up from 3.5% in Q2 2024, amid robust issuance. Green bonds remained the dominant sustainable bond instrument, representing 75.1% of the sustainable bond total at the end of September (**Figure 5**). Most sustainable bonds outstanding in the Indonesian market at the end of September were from the public sector (65.8%), as the Government of Indonesia remains committed to fulfilling its Sustainable Development Goals. Owing to the public sector's active participation, sustainable bond financing in Indonesia is largely concentrated in longer tenors, with bonds carrying maturities of over 5 years comprising 70.6% of outstanding public sector sustainable bonds at the end of September. In contrast, private sector sustainable bonds largely comprised shorter tenors (62.6%). Overall, the size-weighted average tenor of sustainable bonds in Indonesia stood at 8.4 years at the end of Q3 2024.

Figure 4: Investor Profile of Tradable Central Government Bonds

Source: Directorate General of Budget Financing and Risk Management, Ministry of Finance.

Figure 5: Market Profile of Outstanding Sustainable Bonds in Indonesia at the End of September 2024

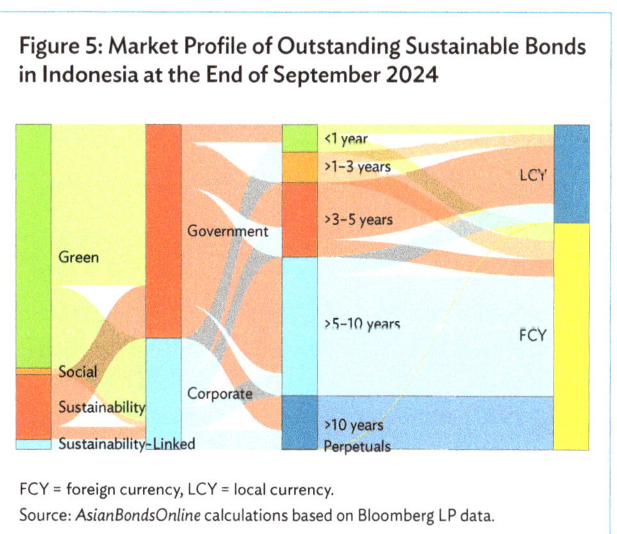

FCY = foreign currency, LCY = local currency.

Source: *AsianBondsOnline* calculations based on Bloomberg LP data.

---

[14] Emerging East Asia is defined to include member states of the Association of Southeast Asian Nations plus the People's Republic of China; Hong Kong, China; and the Republic of Korea.

Republic of Korea

Yield Movements

Local currency (LCY) government bond yields in the Republic of Korea fell for all tenors between 2 September and 31 October. Yields fell an average of 13 basis points (bps) during the review period, with tenors of less than 1 year posting the largest average decline of 28 bps (**Figure 1**). Yields fell ahead of the expected monetary policy easing by the United States Federal Reserve at its 17–18 September meeting, when it ultimately cut the federal funds rate by 50 bps. Moreover, on 11 October, the Bank of Korea cut the base rate by 25 bps to 3.25% amid stable inflation and a slowdown in household debt growth. Inflation eased from 2.0% year-on-year (y-o-y) in August to 1.6% y-o-y and 1.3% y-o-y in September and October, respectively.

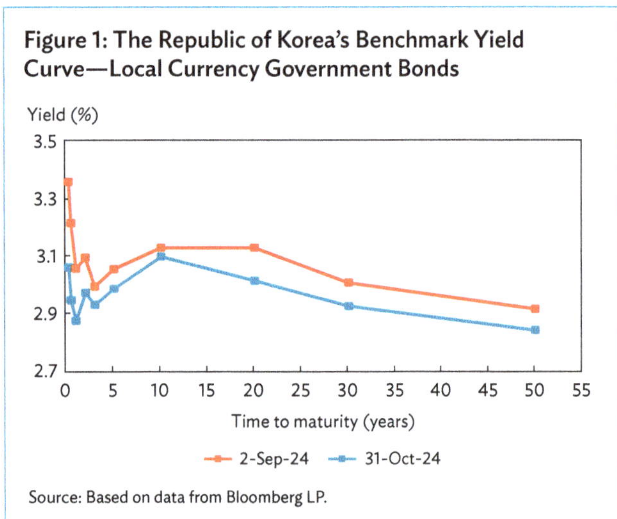

Figure 1: The Republic of Korea's Benchmark Yield Curve—Local Currency Government Bonds

Source: Based on data from Bloomberg LP.

Local Currency Bond Market Size and Issuance

The Republic of Korea's LCY bond market posted marginal growth of 0.01% quarter-on-quarter (q-o-q) in the third quarter (Q3) of 2024, reaching a size of KRW3,292.5 trillion at the end of September. The Republic of Korea remained the second-largest LCY

bond market in emerging East Asia, comprising almost 10% of the regional bond total.[15] The stock of government bonds, which accounted for 38.1% of the total bond market, was barely changed in Q3 2024 from the previous quarter due to reduced issuance. Meanwhile, corporate bonds, which comprised 58.5% of total bonds, rose 0.3% q-o-q in Q3 2024. This was a reversal from the 0.5% q-o-q contraction in the second quarter, as issuance increased during the quarter (**Figure 2**).

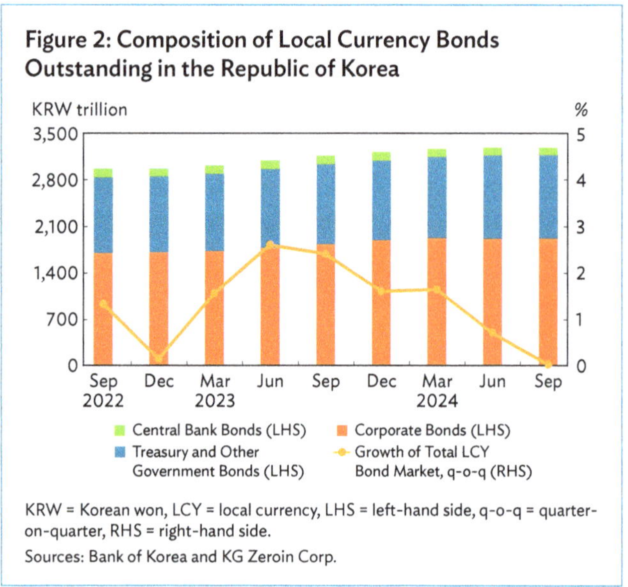

Figure 2: Composition of Local Currency Bonds Outstanding in the Republic of Korea

KRW = Korean won, LCY = local currency, LHS = left-hand side, q-o-q = quarter-on-quarter, RHS = right-hand side.
Sources: Bank of Korea and KG Zeroin Corp.

LCY bond issuance contracted 0.3% q-o-q to KRW241.4 trillion in Q3 2024 driven by reduced issuance of government bonds. Issuance of government bonds contracted 15.6% q-o-q in Q3 2024 as the government borrowed less during the quarter, following its frontloading policy in the first half of the year. Meanwhile, issuance of corporate bonds rebounded in Q3 2024, posting an increase of 7.4% q-o-q, a reversal from the 13.9% q-o-q contraction in the previous quarter (**Figure 3**). Issuance rose as companies took advantage of lower bond yields amid expected rate cuts by both the Bank of Korea and the Federal Reserve.

This market summary was written by Angelica Andrea Cruz, consultant, Economic Research and Development Impact Department, ADB, Manila.
[15] Emerging East Asia is defined to include member states of the Association of Southeast Asian Nations plus the People's Republic of China; Hong Kong, China; and the Republic of Korea.

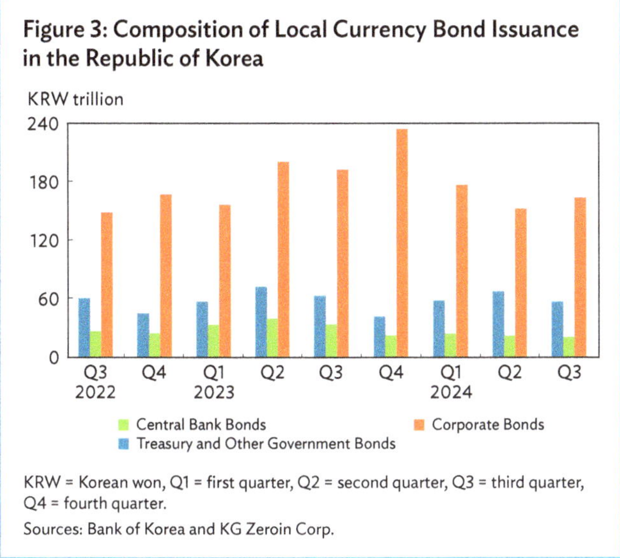

Figure 3: Composition of Local Currency Bond Issuance in the Republic of Korea

KRW = Korean won, Q1 = first quarter, Q2 = second quarter, Q3 = third quarter, Q4 = fourth quarter.

Sources: Bank of Korea and KG Zeroin Corp.

Investor Profile

The Republic of Korea's LCY government bond market continued to have one of the most diverse investor bases in the region at the end of June 2024. The Republic of Korea had the second-lowest Herfindahl–Hirschman Index score in emerging East Asia at the end of June.[16] Insurance companies and pension funds held the largest share of LCY government bonds outstanding at 29.0%. Banks, foreign investors, and other financial institutions had shares of 20.5%, 18.5%, and 16.1%, respectively (**Figure 4**). Meanwhile, the corporate bond market had a less diverse investor base—with almost three-fourths of the market held by only two major investor groups. These include other financial institutions with a share of 42.3%, and insurance companies and pension funds with a collective share of 29.0%. Foreign holdings of corporate bonds remained negligible at the of end June.

Sustainable Bond Market

The Republic of Korea's sustainable bond market at the end of September 2024 mostly comprised government-issued social bonds and private sector green bonds. The Republic of Korea had the second-largest sustainable bond market in emerging East Asia at the end of September with outstanding bonds reaching USD182.6 billion on 1.8% q-o-q growth. Social bonds accounted for 52.3% of the sustainable bond market, of which 70.1% came from the government (**Figure 5**). Green bonds were the next most common type of sustainable bonds at the end of September with a share of 30.1%, mostly issued by the private sector. Nearly 70% of sustainable bonds outstanding carried maturities of less than 3 years, resulting in an overall size-weighted average tenor of 3.1 years. Moreover, over half of the Republic of Korea's sustainable bonds were denominated in Korean won.

Figure 4: Local Currency Bonds Outstanding Investor Profile

Sources: *AsianBondsOnline* and Bank of Korea.

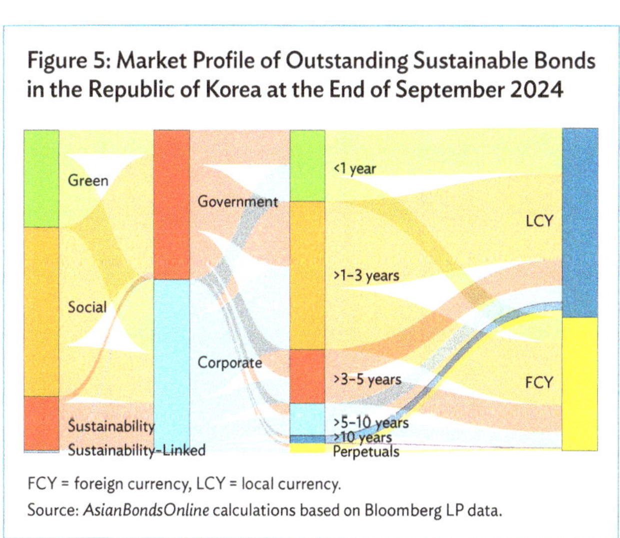

Figure 5: Market Profile of Outstanding Sustainable Bonds in the Republic of Korea at the End of September 2024

FCY = foreign currency, LCY = local currency.

Source: *AsianBondsOnline* calculations based on Bloomberg LP data.

---

[16] The Herfindahl–Hirschman Index is a common measure of market concentration. The index is used to measure the investor profile diversification of the local currency bond market by summing the squared share of each investor group in the bond market.

Malaysia

Yield Movements

Local currency (LCY) government bond yields in Malaysia increased for all tenors between 2 September and 31 October. The LCY government bond yield curve of Malaysia shifted upward during the review period, increasing an average of 12 basis points across all maturities on expectations that Bank Negara Malaysia would hold its policy rate steady for the rest of the year (**Figure 1**). During its meeting on 5 September, as expected, Bank Negara Malaysia left the overnight policy rate unchanged at 3.0% in alignment with current and expected levels of inflation and economic growth.

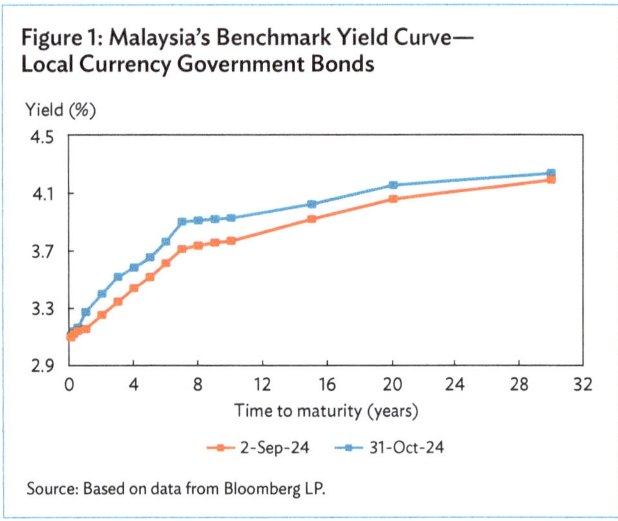

Figure 1: Malaysia's Benchmark Yield Curve—Local Currency Government Bonds

Source: Based on data from Bloomberg LP.

Local Currency Bond Market Size and Issuance

The LCY bond market of Malaysia expanded 0.9% quarter-on-quarter (q-o-q) to reach a size of MYR2.1 trillion at the end of September, with growth in both the corporate and government bond segments. Malaysia's corporate bond segment grew 0.6% q-o-q in the third quarter (Q3) of 2024 due to increased issuance (**Figure 2**). Malaysia's government bond market rose 1.2% q-o-q in Q3 2024, despite a

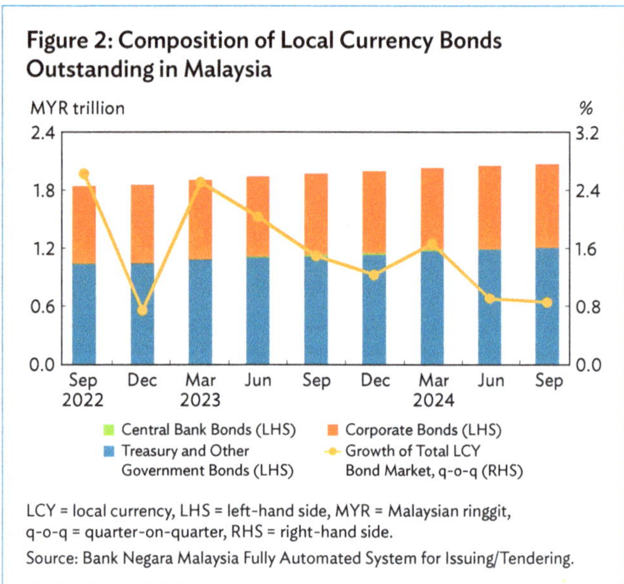

Figure 2: Composition of Local Currency Bonds Outstanding in Malaysia

LCY = local currency, LHS = left-hand side, MYR = Malaysian ringgit, q-o-q = quarter-on-quarter, RHS = right-hand side.
Source: Bank Negara Malaysia Fully Automated System for Issuing/Tendering.

contraction in issuance, on a lower volume of maturities during the quarter. At the end of September, there were no outstanding central bank bills due to the absence of issuance during the quarter. A majority (63.6%) of the LCY bond market comprised *sukuk* (Islamic bonds) at the end of September.

Malaysia's total LCY bond issuance fell 9.6% q-o-q to MYR105.2 billion in Q3 2024 due to reduced issuance of Treasury bills and the absence of any issuance by the central bank. Total government bond issuance decreased 10.9% q-o-q in Q3 2024 as the 4.4% q-o-q increase in the issuance of Malaysian Government Securities and Government Investment Issues was outweighed by the 69.2% q-o-q contraction in the issuance of Treasury bills. The contraction in issuance of central bank bills that started in the fourth quarter of 2023 culminated in zero issuance in Q3 2024 as liquidity factors normalized (**Figure 3**). On the other hand, corporate bond issuance increased 18.2% q-o-q in Q3 2024 following growth of 17.1% q-o-q in the previous quarter. CIMB Islamic Malaysia issued the largest amount of LCY bonds in Q3 2024 with *sukuk* medium-term notes and *sukuk* issuances totaling MYR4.2 billion.

This market summary was written by Justin Adrian Villas, consultant, Economic Research and Development Impact Department, ADB, Manila.

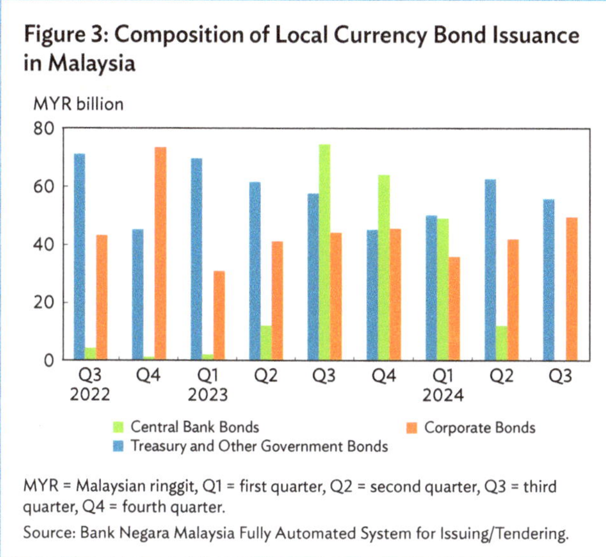

Figure 3: Composition of Local Currency Bond Issuance in Malaysia

MYR = Malaysian ringgit, Q1 = first quarter, Q2 = second quarter, Q3 = third quarter, Q4 = fourth quarter.

Source: Bank Negara Malaysia Fully Automated System for Issuing/Tendering.

Investor Profile

At the end of June, almost 80% of Malaysia's LCY government bonds were held by domestic investors. The largest holdings shares were those of financial institutions and social security institutions at 32.6% and 29.7%, respectively (**Figure 4**). At the end of June, foreign holdings in Malaysia's government bond market fell to 21.4% from 23.1% a year earlier. Among all emerging East Asian LCY bond markets, Malaysia has the largest share of foreign ownership.[17]

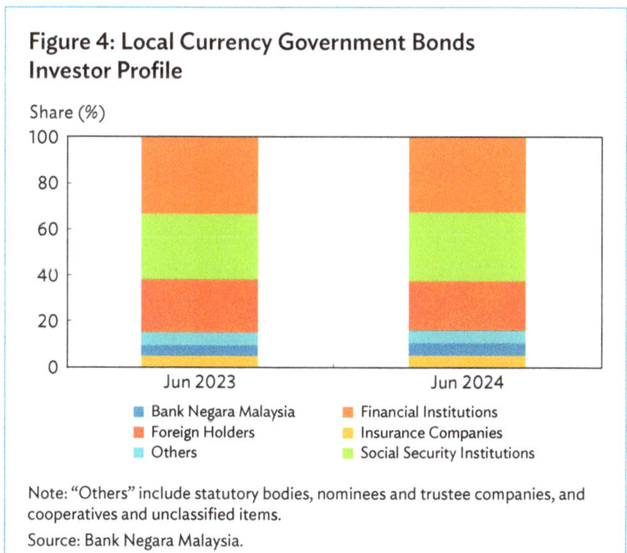

Figure 4: Local Currency Government Bonds Investor Profile

Note: "Others" include statutory bodies, nominees and trustee companies, and cooperatives and unclassified items.

Source: Bank Negara Malaysia.

Sustainable Bond Market

At the end of September, Malaysia's sustainable bond market was dominated by long-term corporate bonds. Malaysia's sustainable bond market totaled USD15.2 billion at the end of September, reflecting 7.0% q-o-q growth in Q3 2024, with a majority of bonds denominated in Malaysian ringgit (83.4%). Of total sustainable bonds outstanding, 73.6% comprised sustainability bonds, followed by green bonds at 18.1% (**Figure 5**). Corporate bonds accounted for 77.0% of outstanding sustainable bonds at the end of September, with over 56.3% of corporate issuances carrying tenors of more than 5 years. While all outstanding sustainable bonds issued by the government carried maturities of more than 5 years, the public sector only comprised 23.0% of total sustainable bonds outstanding. At the end of September, the size-weighted average tenor in Malaysia's sustainable bond market was 8.7 years.

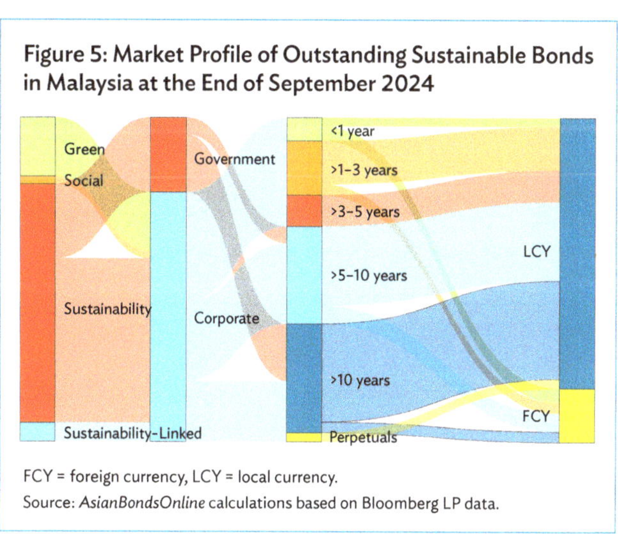

Figure 5: Market Profile of Outstanding Sustainable Bonds in Malaysia at the End of September 2024

FCY = foreign currency, LCY = local currency.

Source: *AsianBondsOnline* calculations based on Bloomberg LP data.

Philippines

Yield Movements

Local currency (LCY) government bond yields in the Philippines fell an average of 33 basis points across all tenors between 2 September and 31 October, driven by the Bangko Sentral ng Pilipinas' (BSP) dovish monetary policy stance (Figure 1). The BSP reduced its overnight reverse repurchase rate by 25 basis points on 15 August and again on 16 October, bringing the main policy rate down to 6.00% amid cooling domestic inflation. Year-on-year inflation slowed to 1.9% in September from 3.3% in August. While inflation rose to 2.3% year-on-year in October, it remained within the government's target range of 2.0%–4.0%.

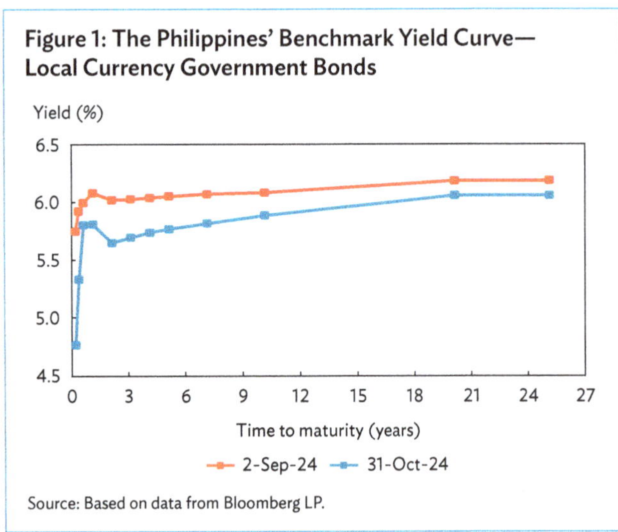

Figure 1: The Philippines' Benchmark Yield Curve—Local Currency Government Bonds

Source: Based on data from Bloomberg LP.

Local Currency Bond Market Size and Issuance

Growth in the LCY bond market accelerated in the third quarter (Q3) of 2024 on robust expansion in all bond segments. Total LCY bonds outstanding reached PHP13.0 trillion at the end of September on accelerated growth of 3.8% quarter-on-quarter (q-o-q), up from 1.9% q-o-q in the second quarter (**Figure 2**). Treasury and other government bonds grew 3.6% q-o-q on increased borrowing amid a high volume of bond maturities during the quarter. The total corporate debt stock rebounded

to expand 3.1% q-o-q in Q3 2024 from the previous quarter's 7.7% q-o-q contraction, as corporates increased their issuance after the BSP's policy easing in August.

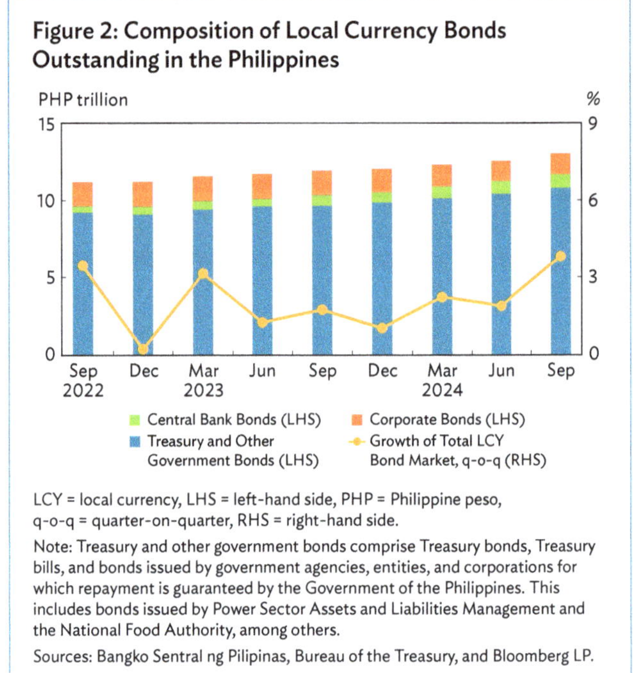

Figure 2: Composition of Local Currency Bonds Outstanding in the Philippines

LCY = local currency, LHS = left-hand side, PHP = Philippine peso, q-o-q = quarter-on-quarter, RHS = right-hand side.
Note: Treasury and other government bonds comprise Treasury bonds, Treasury bills, and bonds issued by government agencies, entities, and corporations for which repayment is guaranteed by the Government of the Philippines. This includes bonds issued by Power Sector Assets and Liabilities Management and the National Food Authority, among others.
Sources: Bangko Sentral ng Pilipinas, Bureau of the Treasury, and Bloomberg LP.

LCY bond issuance rebounded in Q3 2024, propelled by lowered interest rates. Total LCY bond issuance grew 11.0% q-o-q to PHP2.9 trillion in Q3 2024, a reversal from the previous quarter's 15.7% q-o-q contraction (**Figure 3**). Due to the government's increased borrowing amid a large amount of maturities during the quarter, the issuance of Treasury and other government bonds increased 34.0% q-o-q in Q3 2024. Similarly, corporate bond issuance increased more than three-fold to PHP165.4 billion, from PHP43.1 billion in the previous quarter, amid declining borrowing costs. The largest corporate bond issuances during the quarter came from BDO Unibank, which issued a 1.5-year sustainability bond worth PHP55.7 billion, and Bank of the Philippine Islands, which also issued a 1.5-year sustainability bond worth PHP33.7 billion. These issuances represented 33.7% and 20.4% of the Philippines' total corporate issuance in Q3 2024, respectively.

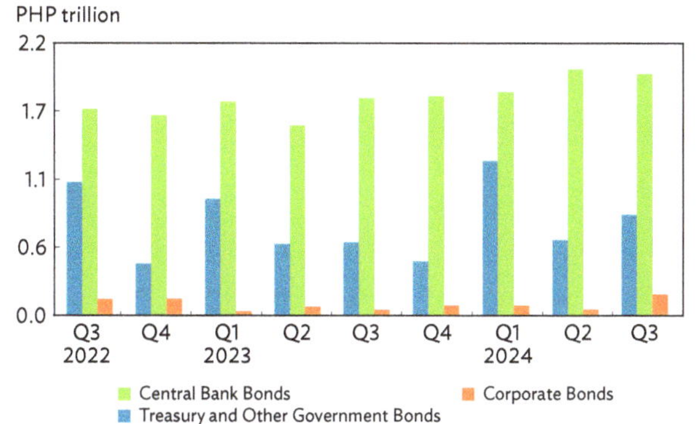

Figure 3: Composition of Local Currency Bond Issuance in the Philippines

PHP trillion

PHP = Philippine peso, Q1 = first quarter, Q2 = second quarter, Q3 = third quarter, Q4 = fourth quarter.

Note: Treasury and other government bonds comprise Treasury bonds, Treasury bills, and bonds issued by government agencies, entities, and corporations for which repayment is guaranteed by the Government of the Philippines. This includes bonds issued by Power Sector Assets and Liabilities Management and the National Food Authority, among others.

Sources: Bangko Sentral ng Pilipinas, Bureau of the Treasury, and Bloomberg LP.

Investor Profile

Banks and investment houses remained the largest investor group in the Philippines' LCY bond market at the end of September. This investor group's holdings share dipped to 45.7% at the end of Q3 2024 from 46.6% a year earlier (**Figure 4**). Contractual savings institutions

and tax-exempt institutions remained the Philippines LCY bond market's second-largest investor group, with its investment holdings share dipping to 30.0% from 32.2% during the same period. The economy's investor profile for LCY government bonds at the end of September 2024 was largely consistent from a year earlier as it remained dominated by these two investor groups.

Sustainable Bond Market

At the end of September, the Philippines' sustainable bond market mainly comprised foreign-currency-denominated sustainability bond instruments. Sustainability bonds accounted for 83.8% of the economy's total sustainable bonds outstanding at the end of Q3 2024 (**Figure 5**). Due to increased issuance by corporates during the quarter, sustainable bonds outstanding grew 20.3% q-o-q to USD10.9 billion at the end of September, about 66.0% of which were foreign-currency denominated. The government and corporate segments each comprised a roughly equal share of the market. The government sector typically issues longer-term sustainable bonds that are denominated in foreign currencies, whereas the private sector prefers issuing sustainable bonds with maturities under 10 years and in local currency. At the end of September, the size-weighted average tenor in the Philippines' sustainable bond market was 12.9 years.

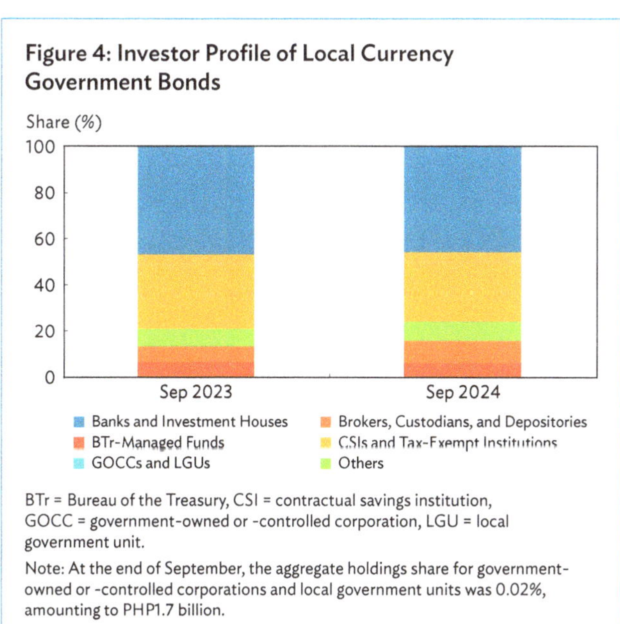

Figure 4: Investor Profile of Local Currency Government Bonds

Share (%)

BTr = Bureau of the Treasury, CSI = contractual savings institution, GOCC = government-owned or -controlled corporation, LGU = local government unit.

Note: At the end of September, the aggregate holdings share for government-owned or -controlled corporations and local government units was 0.02%, amounting to PHP1.7 billion.

Source: Bureau of the Treasury.

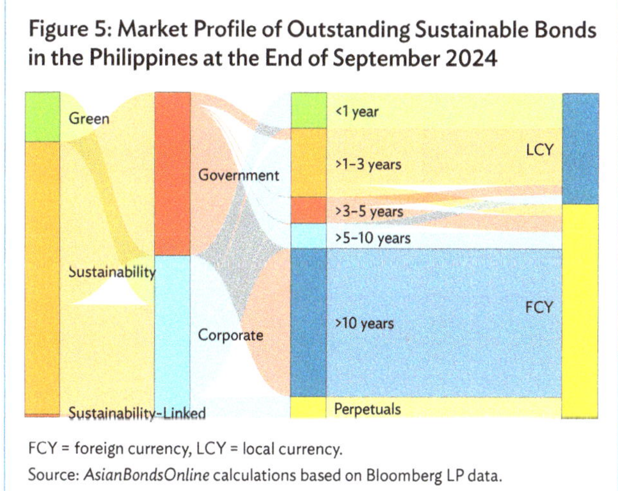

Figure 5: Market Profile of Outstanding Sustainable Bonds in the Philippines at the End of September 2024

FCY = foreign currency, LCY = local currency.

Source: *AsianBondsOnline* calculations based on Bloomberg LP data.

Singapore

Yield Movements

Between 2 September and 31 October, the yield movements of Singapore's local currency (LCY) government bonds were mixed. Yields fell at the short end of the curve but rose for medium- to long-term securities (2-year to 15-year bonds), largely tracking the yield movements of United States Treasuries (**Figure 1**). On the other hand, yields at the very long end (20-year and 30-year bonds) of the curve dipped by an average of 12 basis points due to slowing inflation. On 14 October, the Monetary Authority of Singapore (MAS) decided to keep its monetary policy unchanged, retaining the slope, width, and level (at which it is centered) of the Singapore dollar's nominal effective exchange rate policy band amid a positive economic growth outlook and decreasing inflationary pressure. Singapore's consumer price inflation eased to 2.0% year-on-year in September, down from 2.2% year-on-year in August, well within MAS estimates of 1.5%–2.5% for full-year 2024.

Local Currency Bond Market Size and Issuance

Singapore's LCY bond market grew 1.8% quarter-on-quarter (q-o-q) in the third quarter (Q3) of 2024 to reach a size of SGD836.3 billion at the end of September. Growth in Treasuries moderated to 0.6% q-o-q in Q3 2024 from 7.3% q-o-q in the previous quarter, driven mainly by reduced issuance during the period (**Figure 2**). Central bank bills also grew 4.4% q-o-q, down from the previous quarter's growth of 4.7% q-o-q. Meanwhile, the corporate bond segment contracted 0.7% q-o-q, driven mainly by a decline in issuance during the quarter. The state-owned Housing & Development Board continued to have the largest amount of outstanding LCY corporate bonds at the end of September, amounting to SGD29.0 billion.

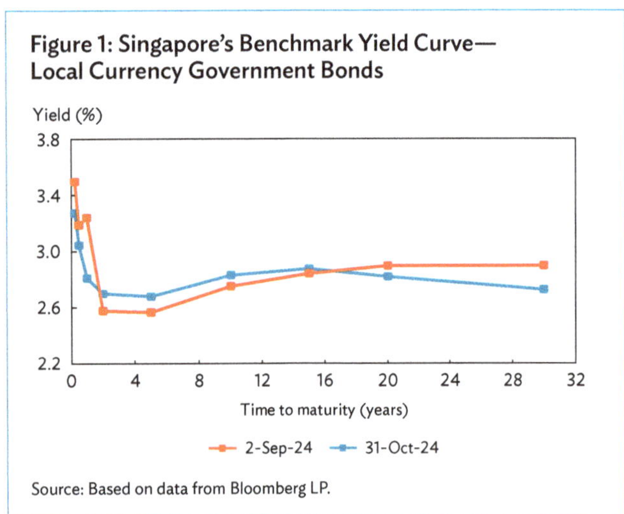

Figure 1: Singapore's Benchmark Yield Curve— Local Currency Government Bonds

Source: Based on data from Bloomberg LP.

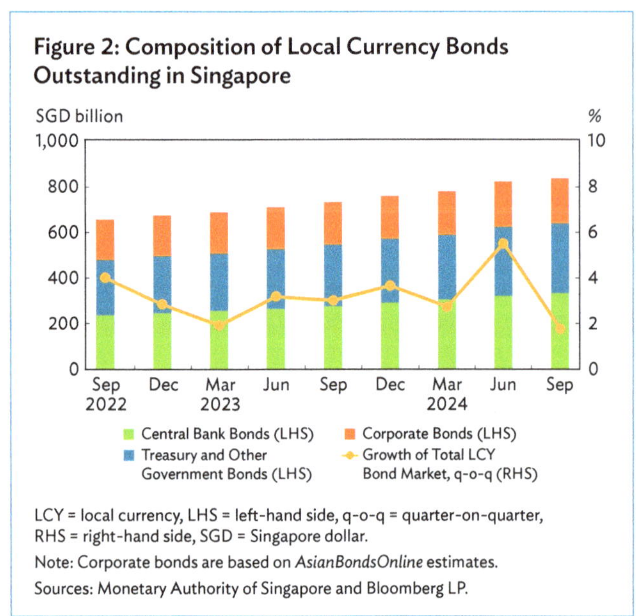

Figure 2: Composition of Local Currency Bonds Outstanding in Singapore

LCY = local currency, LHS = left-hand side, q-o-q = quarter-on-quarter, RHS = right-hand side, SGD = Singapore dollar.
Note: Corporate bonds are based on *AsianBondsOnline* estimates.
Sources: Monetary Authority of Singapore and Bloomberg LP.

This market summary was written by Justin Adrian Villas, consultant, Economic Research and Development Impact Department, ADB, Manila.

LCY bond issuance contracted 3.7% q-o-q in Q3 2024, reversing the previous quarter's growth of 23.2% q-o-q.
Total issuance reached SGD544.7 billion in Q3 2024, with all bond segments posting q-o-q contractions. MAS bills, which accounted for almost 90% of total issuance in Q3 2024, declined 2.1% q-o-q, reversing the 22.8% q-o-q growth in the previous quarter (**Figure 3**). Issuance of Treasury and other government bonds also exhibited a decline of 15.6% q-o-q in Q3 2024, following growth of 27.3% q-o-q in the prior quarter. Corporate bond issuance contracted 22.4% q-o-q in Q3 2024. The largest corporate bond issuer in Q3 2024 was the Housing & Development Board, with issuance of SGD965.0 million, representing 27% of the corporate issuance total during the quarter.

Sustainable Bond Market

Singapore's sustainable bond market is predominantly made up of green bond instruments, which accounted for 82.3% of the total at the end of September. In Q3 2024, sustainable bonds outstanding grew 9.6% q-o-q to reach USD24.5 billion, comprising roughly equal shares of government and corporate bonds (**Figure 4**). At the end of September, 43% of total outstanding sustainable bonds carried tenors of over 10 years, resulting in a size-weighted average tenor of 17.6 years, the longest among emerging East Asian markets.[18] The Government of Singapore was the largest issuer of sustainable bonds during the quarter, having reopened a 50-year green bond amounting to SGD1.5 billion in September.

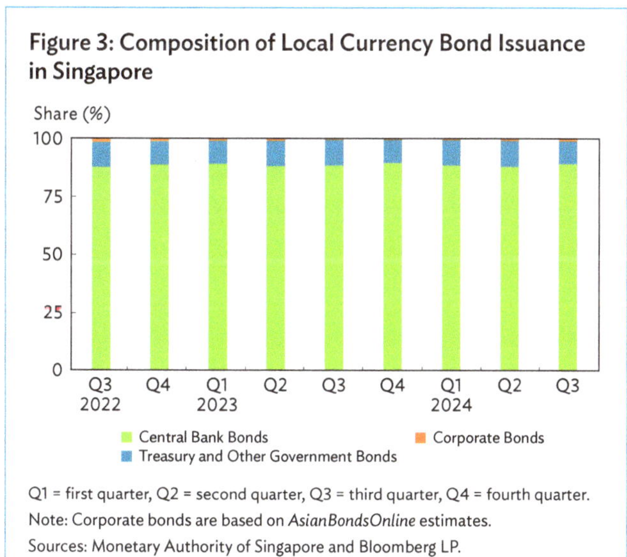

Figure 3: Composition of Local Currency Bond Issuance in Singapore

Q1 = first quarter, Q2 = second quarter, Q3 = third quarter, Q4 = fourth quarter.
Note: Corporate bonds are based on *AsianBondsOnline* estimates.
Sources: Monetary Authority of Singapore and Bloomberg LP.

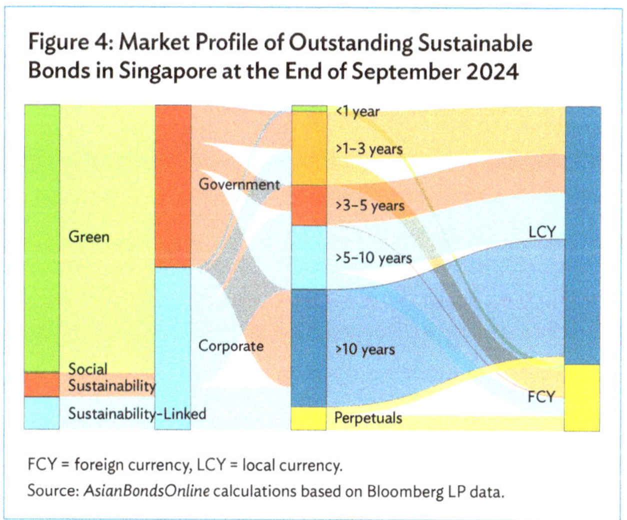

Figure 4: Market Profile of Outstanding Sustainable Bonds in Singapore at the End of September 2024

FCY = foreign currency, LCY = local currency.
Source: *AsianBondsOnline* calculations based on Bloomberg LP data.

---

[18] Emerging East Asia is defined to include member states of the Association of Southeast Asian Nations plus the People's Republic of China; Hong Kong, China; and the Republic of Korea.

Thailand

Yield Movements

Between 2 September and 31 October, Thailand's local currency (LCY) government bond yields edged down amid monetary policy easing by the Bank of Thailand (BOT). Yields fell an average of 12 basis points across all maturities, with the 20-year bond yield posting the steepest drop (**Figure 1**). The decline in yields was primarily driven by the BOT's move to reduce its policy rate by 25 basis points at its 16 October meeting to ease the debt servicing burden for borrowers. The BOT upgraded its gross domestic product growth forecast for 2024 to 2.7% (from its June projection of 2.6%) and trimmed its forecast for average headline inflation in 2024 to 0.5% (from 0.6% in June). Thailand's year-on-year consumer price inflation inched up to 0.8% in October from 0.6% in September and 0.4% in August, but remained below the BOT target of 1.0%–3.0%. Nonetheless, the central bank expects headline inflation to return within its target range by the end of the year.

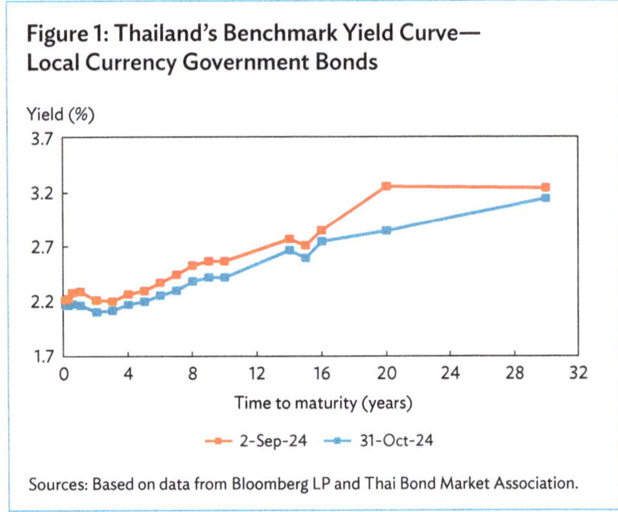

Figure 1: Thailand's Benchmark Yield Curve—Local Currency Government Bonds

Sources: Based on data from Bloomberg LP and Thai Bond Market Association.

Local Currency Bond Market Size and Issuance

Thailand's LCY bond market rebounded in the third quarter (Q3) of 2024, supported by growth in government and BOT bonds. Total LCY bonds outstanding reached a size of THB17.1 trillion at the end of September, rising 1.1% quarter-on-quarter (q-o-q) in Q3 2024 after a nominal contraction of 0.2% q-o-q in the prior quarter (**Figure 2**). The stock of Treasury and other government bonds grew 1.5% q-o-q to THB10.0 trillion as the government continued to issue debt to help finance the its stimulus measures. Outstanding BOT bonds rose to THB2.4 trillion on 5.4% q-o-q growth, supported by robust issuance. Meanwhile, outstanding corporate bonds fell 1.8% q-o-q to THB4.7 trillion as issuance contracted amid political uncertainties brought about by the recent change in the Thai government. Thailand's bond market continued to be dominated by Treasury and government bonds, which comprised 58.7% of the total LCY bond stock at the end of September.

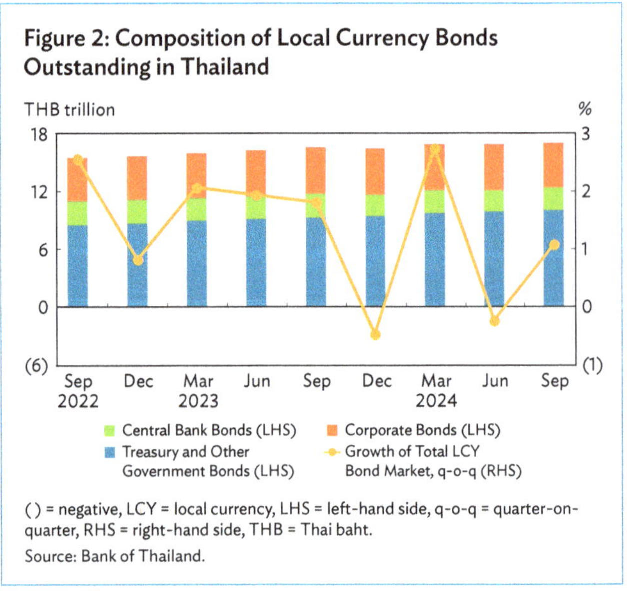

Figure 2: Composition of Local Currency Bonds Outstanding in Thailand

( ) = negative, LCY = local currency, LHS = left-hand side, q-o-q = quarter-on-quarter, RHS = right-hand side, THB = Thai baht.
Source: Bank of Thailand.

Weak corporate bond sales amid elevated political risks capped overall growth in LCY bond issuance in Q3 2024. Issuance of LCY bonds fell 2.6% q-o-q to THB2.2 trillion in Q3 2024 (**Figure 3**). Corporate bond sales amounted to THB0.4 trillion in Q3 2024, down 19.8% q-o-q as political uncertainties surrounding the change in government dampened investor confidence. Energy and utility companies were the top issuers in Q3 2024, with aggregate issuance of THB48.7 billion, comprising 12.2% of total corporate bond sales.

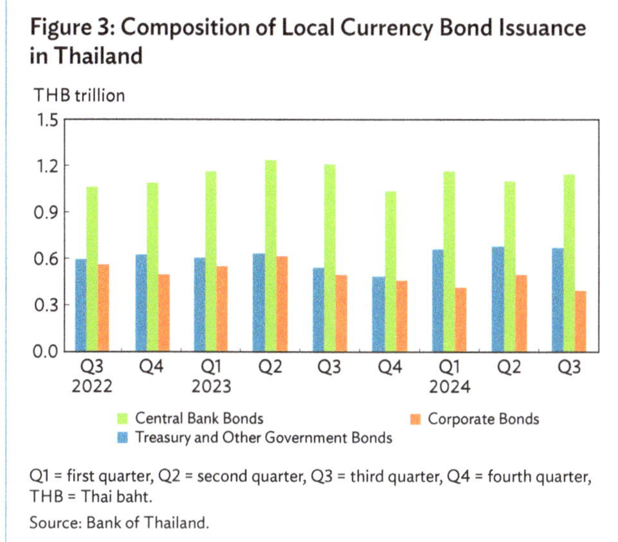

Figure 3: Composition of Local Currency Bond Issuance in Thailand

Q1 = first quarter, Q2 = second quarter, Q3 = third quarter, Q4 = fourth quarter, THB = Thai baht.
Source: Bank of Thailand.

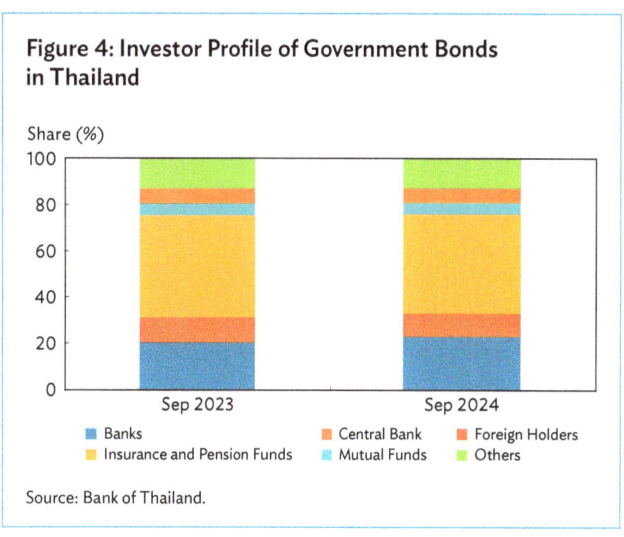

Figure 4: Investor Profile of Government Bonds in Thailand

Source: Bank of Thailand.

Meanwhile, Treasury and other government bond issuance inched down 1.8% q-o-q in Q3 2024 as debt sales moderated. The government continued to issue debt to finance its fiscal deficit, but at a lesser volume than the prior quarter. In contrast, issuance of BOT bonds posted robust growth of 4.7% q-o-q, totaling THB1.1 billion.

Investor Profile

Insurance and pension funds and banks remained the primary holders of LCY government bonds at the end of September. LCY government bond holdings of the top two investor groups rose to 66.2% of total outstanding LCY government bonds at the end of September from 65.0% a year earlier (**Figure 4**). In contrast, foreign holdings inched down to a share of 10.1% from 10.9% during the same period as heightened political risks dampened foreign demand for Thai sovereign bonds.

Sustainable Bond Market

Thailand's sustainable bond market reached a size of USD22.3 billion at the end of September. Sustainability bonds continued to be the predominant bond type, comprising 67.0% of the sustainable bond market, followed by green bonds with a 20.2% share (**Figure 5**). A majority (68.4%) of outstanding sustainable bonds were government-issued instruments, which tend to have long-term maturities. As a result, the size-weighted

average tenor of outstanding sustainable bonds at the end of September was 8.9 years, and over 64% of total outstanding sustainable bonds had remaining maturities of longer than 10 years at the end of September. Sustainable bonds in Thailand are primarily issued in Thai baht. Among all emerging East Asian markets, Thailand had the highest share of LCY-denominated sustainable bonds at the end of September with 98.1%.[19] For the rest of emerging East Asian markets, the share of LCY-denominated bonds to total sustainable bonds ranged from 21.9% to 83.4%. New issuances of sustainable bonds in Q3 2024 totaled USD1.3 billion of sustainability, social, green, and sustainability-linked instruments.

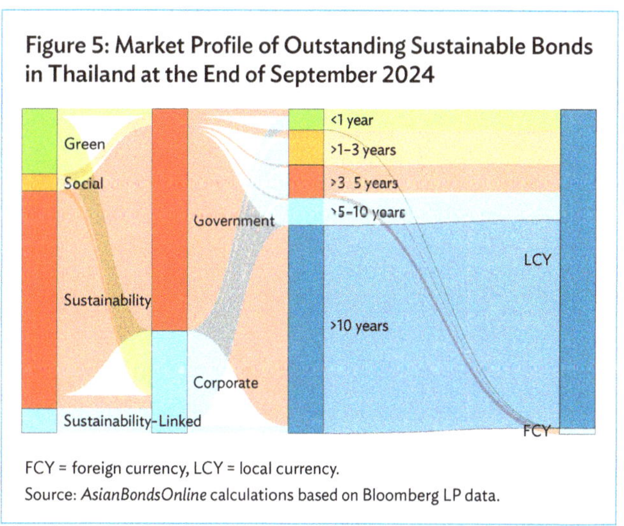

Figure 5: Market Profile of Outstanding Sustainable Bonds in Thailand at the End of September 2024

FCY = foreign currency, LCY = local currency.
Source: *AsianBondsOnline* calculations based on Bloomberg LP data.

<hr>

[19] Emerging East Asia is defined to include member states of the Association of Southeast Asian Nations plus the People's Republic of China; Hong Kong, China; and the Republic of Korea.

Viet Nam

Yield Movements

Between 2 September and 31 October, local currency (LCY) government bond yields in Viet Nam fell an average of 2 basis points across all tenors, propelled by the State Bank of Vietnam's (SBV) accommodative monetary policy stance (Figure 1). On 17 October, the SBV signaled its openness to reducing the policy rate to support the economy, as the government aims to lift annual economic growth above 7.0% in 2024. Viet Nam's economy grew a stronger-than-expected 7.4% year-on-year in the third quarter (Q3) of 2024, up from 6.9% year-on-year in the previous quarter, despite the destruction caused by Typhoon Yagi in September. Furthermore, the SBV reduced its interest rate for open market operations by 25 basis points each on 5 August and 17 September, bringing the rate down to 4.00% in order to support businesses and encourage borrowing.

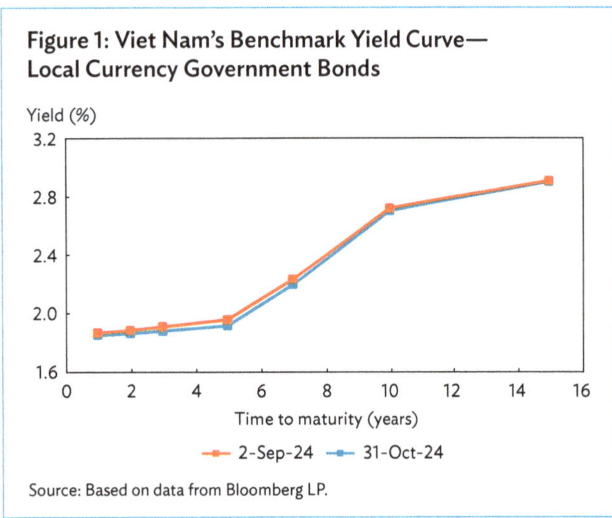

Figure 1: Viet Nam's Benchmark Yield Curve— Local Currency Government Bonds

Source: Based on data from Bloomberg LP.

Local Currency Bond Market Size and Issuance

Total LCY bonds outstanding grew 3.1% quarter-on-quarter (q-o-q) to reach VND3,010.0 trillion at the end of Q3 2024, supported by strong issuance. Treasury and other government bonds outstanding grew 5.3% q-o-q in Q3 2024 to VND2,171.0 trillion, while the total corporate debt stock rebounded strongly with growth of 8.4% q-o-q, reversing the previous quarter's contraction of 0.5% q-o-q (**Figure 2**). The banking and property sectors are the two largest issuers in the economy's LCY bond market, comprising 60.3% and 21.3%, respectively, of total corporate bonds outstanding at the end of Q3 2024.

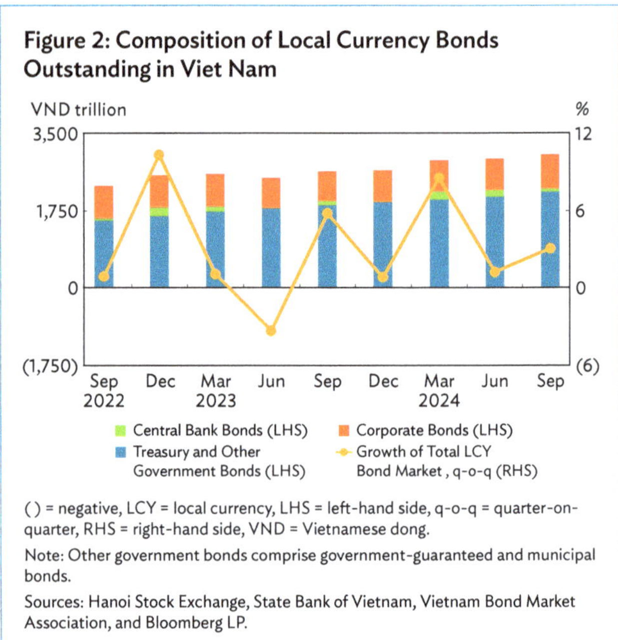

Figure 2: Composition of Local Currency Bonds Outstanding in Viet Nam

( ) = negative, LCY = local currency, LHS = left-hand side, q-o-q = quarter-on-quarter, RHS = right-hand side, VND = Vietnamese dong.
Note: Other government bonds comprise government-guaranteed and municipal bonds.
Sources: Hanoi Stock Exchange, State Bank of Vietnam, Vietnam Bond Market Association, and Bloomberg LP.

LCY bond issuance grew 35.0% q-o-q in Q3 2024 amid lowered interest rate in open market operations. Issuance of Treasury and other government bonds grew 51.0% q-o-q, reversing the previous quarter's 4.9% q-o-q contraction (**Figure 3**). Total corporate bond issuance also grew 39.3% q-o-q in Q3 2024, extending the 268.4% q-o-q growth in the preceding quarter. The banking sector remained the key driver of issuance in Viet Nam's LCY corporate bond market—representing 83.6% of the quarterly total—as financial institutions continued to raise capital amid improved credit growth. The property sector, which accounted for 12.4% of the corporate issuance total in Q3 2024, remained the second-largest issuer of corporate bonds, as property companies sought capital amid lingering pressure from debt repayments and bond maturities.

This market summary was written by Jeremy Grace Ilustrisimo, consultant, Economic Research and Development Impact Department, ADB, Manila.

Figure 3: Composition of Local Currency Bond Issuance in Viet Nam

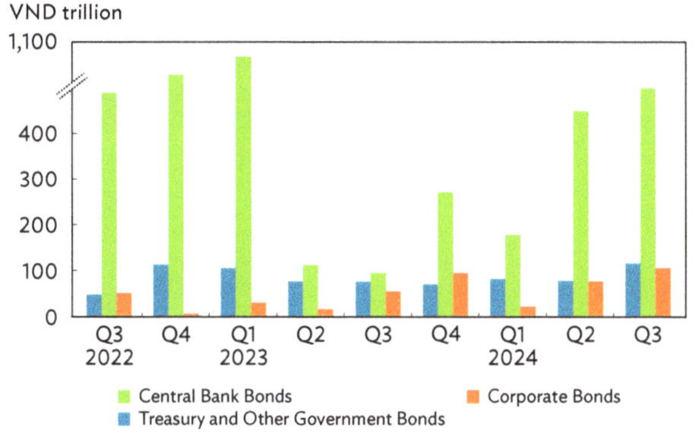

Q1 = first quarter, Q2 = second quarter, Q3 = third quarter, Q4 = fourth quarter, VND = Vietnamese dong.
Note: Other government bonds comprise government-guaranteed and municipal bonds.
Sources: Hanoi Stock Exchange, State Bank of Vietnam, Vietnam Bond Market Association, and Bloomberg LP.

Investor Profile

Insurance firms and banks remained the predominant holders of outstanding LCY government bonds at the end of September. Collectively, these two investor groups held 99.2% of the total LCY government debt stock at the end of Q3 2024 (**Figure 4**). Insurance firms, the largest investor group, slightly increased their holdings share to 59.8% from 59.7% the previous year. Conversely, banks saw their holdings share dip to 39.4% from 39.9% over the

Figure 4: Profile of the Two Dominant Investors for Local Currency Government Bonds

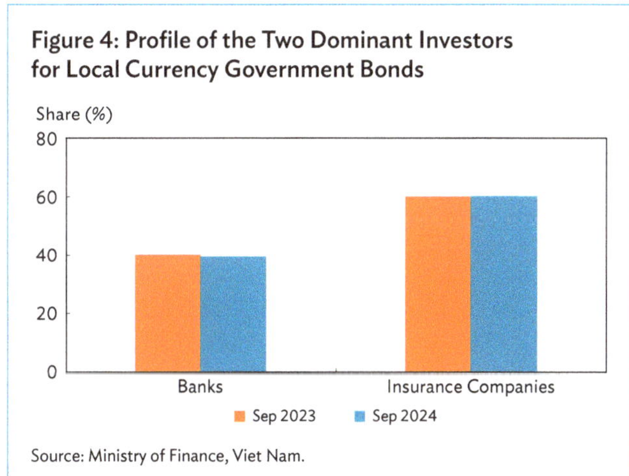

Source: Ministry of Finance, Viet Nam.

same period. This high concentration of just two investor groups led to Viet Nam having the least diversified investor profile in emerging East Asia and the highest Herfindahl–Hirschman Index score in the region at the end of September.[20]

Sustainable Bond Market

Viet Nam's sustainable bond market mainly comprises foreign-currency-denominated green and sustainability bond instruments issued solely by corporates. The economy's sustainable bond market totaled USD0.8 billion at the end of September (**Figure 5**). Green bonds accounted for 46.9% of the market, while sustainability bonds represented 53.1%. Over 78.0% of total sustainable bonds outstanding at the end of September were denominated in a foreign currency and carried tenors of 3 years or less, resulting in a size-weighted average tenor of 2.7 years.

Figure 5: Market Profile of Outstanding Sustainable Bonds in Viet Nam at the End of September 2024

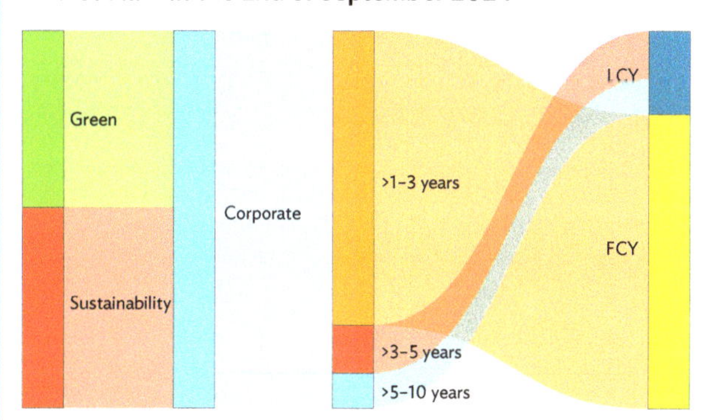

FCY = foreign currency, LCY = local currency.
Source: *AsianBondsOnline* calculations based on Bloomberg LP data.

---

[20] Emerging East Asia is defined to include member states of the Association of Southeast Asian Nations plus the People's Republic of China; Hong Kong, China; and the Republic of Korea. The Herfindahl–Hirschman Index is a common measure of market concentration. The index is used to measure the investor profile diversification of the local currency bond market by summing the squared share of each investor group in the bond market.